GROWING ROSES

Janet Cheriton

CASSELL

Dedication

This book is dedicated to Allan G. Scott, M.B.E., A.H.R.I.H., and
President Emeritus of the National Rose Society of New Zealand.
He is a gentle, inspirational man who grows wonderful roses.
I am proud to call him my friend.

Cassell Publishers Limited
Villiers House, 41/47 Strand
London WC2N 5JE

First published in Great Britain 1995
in association with
David Bateman Limited
'Golden Heights'
32/34 View Road
Glenfield, Auckland 10
New Zealand

Distributed in the United States by Sterling Publishing Co. Inc,
387 Park Avenue South, New York, NY 10016, USA

British Library Cataloguing in Publication Data
A catalogue record for this book is available from the British
Library

ISBN 0-304-34532-6

Printed in Hong Kong by Colorcraft Ltd

Contents

INTRODUCTION

Given a few basic guidelines, anyone can grow wonderful roses; indeed, it is very difficult to prevent roses from growing and flowering. It is in the nature of roses to flower, and the gardener can encourage this by good management techniques. After all, wild species of roses have been growing for some 32 million years without our assistance, so we can safely assume that they will continue to do so.

There are no mysteries or secrets to good rose growing. Given the right growing conditions, roses will respond by producing abundant blooms to delight the gardener, whether experienced or a complete novice.

Give roses a sunny, well-drained position in any reasonable soil, and supply them with adequate water and food. Allow free air circulation around and through the plants, and practise good garden hygiene to help protect against pests and diseases. If your garden grows a variety of weeds well, then it can grow roses well too.

Roses have existed for at least 32 million years, as fossil remains in the Northern hemisphere can testify. That the genus *Rosa* has survived to the present day is testament to its hardiness and adaptability in all soil types and in nearly all climates. It is probable that this hardiness and adaptability is in part responsible for the popularity of roses. Certainly their colour, fragrance and form have delighted people throughout the centuries and these same attributes well qualify the rose for the accolade of "Queen of Flowers".

It is a matter of historical record that roses were popular in the ancient civilisations of Egypt, Rome and Greece. The historian Herodotus (484-424 BC) refers to roses being grown by the legendary King Midas of Crete. The Greek poetess Sappho wrote of roses in the sixth century BC and the virtues of the rose have since been extolled by such luminaries as Omar Khayyam, Geoffrey Chaucer and William Shakespeare.

The recent history of roses is firmly linked with people. The flower forms part of the mythology and religion of many countries and faiths, being featured in the writings of ancient China, and having a place in the Moslem, Hindu, Buddhist and Christian faiths. More than any other flower in history, the rose, and the love of the rose, transcend the boundaries of man's colour, race and creed.

Roses probably became popular in Europe after they were brought back from the Middle East by the Crusaders who chose to recognise in the early, five-petalled rose, the five wounds of the crucified Christ. Many of those same five-petalled varieties may still be grown by today's rose lovers. That these roses are still available today is a tribute to the adaptability of the genus, as well as a tribute to those who have continued to propagate and grow these versatile plants that bring so much history, beauty, variety and fragrance to our gardens. Originally a Northern hemisphere native, the rose has adapted well to the Southern hemisphere, where it grows and thrives in abundance, proving once again its incredible adaptability.

And still we grow roses! Bigger, smaller, more varied in colour, more floriferous, sometimes more fragrant, different in form, but, for all that, still identifiably roses; the roses that Omar Khayyam knew, that Sappho knew, and that we continue to love more than any other plant in our brief history. Each rose is unique in its own special way and today's roses are as beautiful and as much revered as any that have gone before. The history of humankind is inextricably intertwined with the rose, to the benefit of both.

'Old Blush' (China)

Chapter 1

OLD-FASHIONED ROSES

'Souvenir de St Anne's' (Bourbon)

IT is a task fraught with difficulty to define precisely what is meant by the term 'old-fashioned roses'. Generally, however, they are defined by their class rather than by specific, named varieties or cultivars (varieties which have arisen in cultivation rather than in the wild). In fact, many individual cultivars in some classes are of comparatively recent origin, and so would not qualify as old fashioned if limits such as the year of introduction were used. Thus, the roses described here are defined as old-fashioned because of the class to which they belong.

Old-fashioned roses are an incredibly varied group, ranging in size from the enormous rambling roses that adorn walls to minute, dwarf growers suited to growing in the smallest pot. Similarly fragrance is variable, not least due to growing conditions.

The colour of most of the old-fashioneds is muted in comparison with some modern cultivars, and they are often chosen for their gen-

tler colours and softer growth shapes. Many of these roses are 'once flowering'; that is, they will bloom in spring or summer, but will not flower again until the following year. However, many are 'remontant' or 'repeat flowering', and will bear two or more crops of blooms until winter closes them down for the season. This factor needs to be borne in mind when selecting old-fashioned roses, and it would be wise to obtain detailed advice from a local specialist grower as to how a specific rose will grow in any given district, as performance of individual cultivars will vary enormously according to climate and soil type.

Species/Wild roses

These are the oldest classes of roses, and many bear flowers of simple, single form. They are related to the first wild plants that flourished in the Northern hemisphere before the advent of man. In this group are roses native to Asia, Africa and Europe; many of them are fragrant, but flower size and colour vary greatly.

Growth habit is also variable and is to a certain extent influenced by climate. Obviously over time, a rose growing in a temperate climate will surpass in size the same cultivar growing in a climate where hard winters cut it to the ground each year. Sizes given throughout the text are for roses grown outdoors in temperate areas, so adjustments need to be made according to local climatic conditions.

Some species and wild roses are once flowering, others will repeat flower. In this class are many roses whose seed pods or heps are so attractive as to rival the flowers for display. *R. rubiginosa* (syn. *R. eglanteria*), the Sweetbriar rose, has foliage strongly redolent of apples.

Very popular in this class is *R. laevigata*, the Cherokee rose, which has excellent disease resistance, and bears large, single, white flowers with prominent yellow stamens. The fragrance is wonderful, making us yearn for more than just the one profuse blooming.

Clear, bright yellow flowers identify the fragrant *R. xanthina spontanea*, or Canary bird, the almost stemless flowers appearing on attractive, thorny canes.

Gallicas

These roses have been used medicinally since Roman times because of their rich fragrance, considered to be beneficial in the treatment of many illnesses. *R. gallica officinalis*, the Apothecary's rose, was one renowned for its value as a medicine. The petals of this rose retain their fragrance well, even after drying.

Many of the roses grown by the Empress Josephine of France were Gallicas, and Josephine herself may have been responsible for their popularity as garden plants.

They are hardy roses, generally of compact growth habit, but may sometimes throw out

Above: Canary bird (species)

Opposite: R. laevigata, the Cherokee rose

Below: R. gallica officinalis (Gallica)

Above: 'Cardinal de Richelieu' (Gallica)

Above: 'Duchesse de Montebello' (Gallica)

a long cane which droops gracefully with the weight of the flowers it bears. In general, Gallicas are lightly thorned and flower just once in the season, but many are gloriously full petalled and rich looking. They are the epitome of everything that we think of when we think of old-fashioned roses.

If striped roses appeal to you, then you must grow Rosa Mundi (*R. g. versicolor*), striped red, white and pink, and beautifully fragrant.

Damasks

It is probable that Damask roses grew in the Middle East long before humans appeared on the scene. While their precise origins are uncertain, they were mentioned in the writings of Virgil, and were grown widely in Italy as well as the rest of Europe early in the sixteenth century.

Their fragrant flowers were widely used in perfumes, and it is from Damasks that we get attar of roses. The making of attar of roses became an important industry in many of the countries of the former Soviet Union, as well as India, France, Morocco and Egypt.

Lax growth is a characteristic of many of the Damasks, and they are strong-growing plants, often with very large thorns. The single flowering is followed by decorative, elongated heps of unique beauty. Probably introduced into Europe by the Crusaders, almost all Damasks are very fragrant, and were certainly grown in ancient Greece, Persia and Rome.

'Madame Hardy' is a much admired and widely grown member of this class with fragrant flowers on a tall-growing plant. The blooms open palest pink fading to white, and have a green button eye. 'La Ville de Bruxelles' has very fragrant, double flowers of clear pink, with a quartered shape and a central button eye.

Albas

Another very old class, the Albas were grown

Above: 'Rose de Rescht' (Damask)

Below: 'Madame Hardy' (Damask)

in ancient Rome, and like the Gallicas they were widely used for medicinal purposes throughout the Middle Ages and beyond. The plants are delicate looking, belying their hardy constitutions, and they can become very large plants, so may not be the choice for gardeners with little space at their disposal. Albas will even flourish in poor soils, and so are valuable for that characteristic alone, disregarding their generous fragrance. The flowers are normally soft coloured, from white through creams and palest pinks. Unlike most roses, Albas have been found to flower well in shaded positions, a bonus for the gardener who yearns for roses but can provide little sun.

When grown closely, Albas can form impenetrable hedges and some of the taller cultivars may be trained as climbers, adding to their inestimable value in the garden.

'Maxima', the Jacobite rose or Great white rose, is breathtakingly beautiful in creamy-white, with semi-double flowers that are very fragrant. Celestial *(R. alba celestia)* is another

classic in the class, bearing open, cupped blooms of softest pink.

Centifolias

Another class with its origins obscured, the Centifolias are reputed to have been the roses grown in the garden of King Midas. These 'roses with a hundred petals' are often known as cabbage roses because of their character-istic shape and fullness.

The plants are lax growers, well endowed with thorns, and the growing canes will arch gracefully if left to their own devices, due to the weight of the flowers. This is most appeal-ing if space permits. Indeed, to cut Centifolias back hard is to spoil the very reason for which they are grown — their natural, arch-ing shape.

'Fantin Latour' is a popular member of the class, growing to around 1 m, and bearing cupped, wide-opening blooms of palest pink,

'Paul Ricault' (Centifolia)

deeper in the centre. The blooms have a rich fragrance.

But the Centifolia class has another member whose charms must not be overlooked, and that is 'Chapeau de Napoléon' ('Cristata'), its unique buds giving the appearance of a three-cornered hat because of the moss-like growth that adorns them. The flowers emerge fully double and clearest pink with an irresistible fragrance. Surely enough compensation for its blooming just once in a season!

Moss roses

Originating from Centifolias by an aberration of growth, the Mosses are named for the appearance of their mossy sepals, and date from the seventeenth century. Their ancestry is mixed, resulting in a wide variety of flower shapes within the class. Some are once flow-

'Commandant Beaurepaire' (Bourbon)

'Comte de Chambord' (Portland)

ering and others will reliably repeat flower, with most being fragrant.

'James Mitchell' bears greenish-brown moss covering the buds, which open to soft, pinkish-mauve blooms, with a tiny 'button eye'. 'Quatre Saisons Blanc Mousseaux' has brownish moss and delicate white buds that open in a very loose shape.

Portlands

With China roses in their ancestry, the Portlands, originating in the mid-nineteenth century, inherited the ability to repeat flower. The plants are sturdy, generally fragrant, with a compact growth habit. Few now remain in cultivation, but those that do have a charm all their own and most bear double blooms.

'Jacques Cartier' is hard to resist, with clear pink blooms, fading to palest pink as they age, and a strong fragrance. 'Comte de Chambord' is a soft pinkish-mauve, with fully double, fragrant flowers.

Bourbons

The Bourbon roses originated on the Île de Bourbon, now known as Réunion, possibly as a hybrid between a China rose and the 'Autumn Damask' *(Damascena bifera)*. Almost all of the Bourbons repeat flower reliably, with sumptuous, fully double blooms, cupped and very fragrant. The growth of the Bourbons is variable, from small, compact plants, to larger cultivars with a lax growth habit. Most are sturdy, vigorous growers.

A personal favourite in this class is 'La Reine Victoria' — almost too beautiful to be true. The blooms are cupped, mid-pink, and nes-

'Variegata di Bologna' (Bourbon)

eighteenth century, these roses have flourished in China for many thousands of years. Their significance at the time of introduction was their ability to reliably repeat flower, and this characteristic was, and still is, much admired by rose lovers. Add to this the fact that Chinas are amongst the earliest of roses to flower in spring, and often continue flowering into early winter in mild districts, and you have the formula for what must have been seen at the time in Europe as perfect roses. The Chinas have lost none of their appeal through the passage of time.

The growth habit of the China roses is much lighter than that of the previous classes described, but don't let that fool you into thinking these roses are fragile plants. They are much tougher than they look, and will delight you with their soft colours that blend perfectly with other flowers in a mixed planting.

'Mutabilis' is a must in this class, with single, buff-coloured flowers turning pink and reddish-bronze with age. A large bush of this rose has been described as reminiscent of a thousand coloured butterflies all landing at once! 'Anna Maria de Montravel' is a small, compact rose, often used for edging or grown in a small pot. The tiny, white blooms appear in fragrant clusters throughout the season.

tled in against the light green foliage. Fragrant? Oh, yes!

But for unique appeal 'Variegata di Bologna' cannot be overlooked, on account of its fragrant white-and-cerise striped blooms.

Boursalts

This is now only a small, but distinct, group of roses. One of the attractions of the Boursalts is their almost thornless canes. Grow them in a sheltered position, as they are not keen to 'tough it out' in exposed gardens, but the sight of a well-grown Boursalt, with its long canes trained to climb, is truly memorable. The only drawback is the brief flowering season, but then most flowering shrubs have this same drawback.

'Amadis' is a charming rose with deep crimson blooms fading to purple as they age.

Chinas

Although only introduced into Europe in the

Noisettes

Another class with China roses in their ancestry, the Noisette blooms have an appealing delicacy, belying the vigour of the plants. Most Noisettes are climbing in habit, and prefer a warm growing position with some shelter to be at their best. Amongst the best of the Noisettes is 'Céline Forestier' because of the spicy fragrance that emanates from the pink-centred, creamy-yellow blooms.

Teas

The Tea roses have unique, glossy foliage that adds to their undeniable appeal. The fragrance of the blooms may have given rise to the name, as some early writers alluded to the fragrance as resembling that of a freshly opened packet of China tea. Another appeal of the Teas is their wide colour range and profuse early blooming. They tend to have later blooms too, but it is that first flush of blooms that characterises the class. The Teas do best in a temperate climate and will grow into much larger plants in such areas.

They can be found in both climbing and bush forms, and are sturdy, reliable plants, tolerant of some neglect. They are not vigorous growers, however, and so are suitable for small gardens and container growing.

For a memorable performance from a Tea rose it is hard to go past the lovely 'Mrs. Herbert Stevens', with its huge, drooping blooms of purest white. It is magical grown over an arch or framework close to living areas where

it can show off its very fragrant, early spring blooms to greatest advantage. 'Lorraine Lee' is a Tea rose to treasure. Tolerant of hot and dry situations, its clear pink buds open to loosely formed flowers with an unforgettable fragrance. Both 'Lorraine Lee' and 'Mrs. Herbert Stevens' are available in bush and climbing forms. In mild climates, both will bloom in late winter and through early spring when other roses are just beginning to shoot.

If you become addicted to Tea roses, which is highly likely after growing one or two, be sure to get a plant of the soft apricot 'Lady Hillingdon', another fragrant charmer.

Hybrid Perpetuals

These are vigorous growers which can become very large plants in mild climates. They are also remontant, bearing more blooms after the initial flowering. Many are upright in habit, and make a wonderful sight if the long, sprawling canes are pegged

'Lady Hillingdon' (Tea)

down, when blooms will appear along their length.

The flowers are really opulent, full and fragrant, and the buds were much admired and exhibited in rose shows in the nineteenth century. Allow for large growth in mild climates for Hybrid Perpetuals to show off to best advantage, but in colder areas, the plants may be pruned to a more restrained shape.

'Reine des Violettes' is one of the more restrained growers, with double, velvety-purple flowers and a button eye. But if it's Hybrid Perpetual in all its glory that you are after, then 'General Jacqueminot', with its loosely cupped, deep crimson blooms and truly overpowering fragrance is a rose that you must have.

Rugosas

These roses must be the most beautiful, toughest and undemanding of any rose on Earth. They grew in Asia many thousands of

'Prince Camille de Rohan' (Hybrid Perpetual)

years ago and were not introduced into Europe until the late-eighteenth century. At that time, they were not favoured for exhibiting in shows, as Hybrid Perpetuals were in vogue, and so they did not become very popular. This may have been in part due to their extremely prickly canes, and Rugosas are very prickly customers!

But what other roses could be used with absolute certainty of flowering on the motor-way verges of England, in some of the coldest parts of Canada, and in the almost pure sand and heat of parts of Western Australia? And how beautiful they are with their crepe-papery blooms unfurling from long, tapered buds. They flower and flower, attracting bees to pollinate them and many bear heps like no others, fat and red and shiny, and the flowers keep on coming as the ones before them set their heps. Rugosas are so reliable under all conditions that in many countries they are used as understocks for budding. The foliage of Rugosas is leathery-looking and deepest green, and the plants just laugh off any hint of the fungal diseases that often beset other roses.

If you have space for just one Rugosa in your garden, it should be *R. rugosa* 'Alba', with its wide open, single blooms of purest white, opening from slender pink buds, spilling its fragrance all around. Each flower's life is fleeting, but fresh flowers appear each day until winter's approach breaks the spell of the Rugosas' magic.

Hybrid Musks

For ample fragrance and strong constitutions, you can't do better than the cluster-flowering Hybrid Musks, at home in cold climates as well as temperate regions. They repeat flower rapidly, the plants are vigorous, and they can be shaped to suit, whether your choice is for a shrubby shape, long, arching canes, or a rose to climb trees with very little help. They are magnificent for mass effect as the many flowers open together on the strong canes, and they can be trained along fences and trellises, or draped gracefully over banks. Hybrid Musks also blend well with annuals and perennials in a mixed border, and can be pruned to shape as desired.

Many colours are available in this class; the

R. rugosa 'Alba' (Rugosa)

'Moonlight' (Hybrid Musk)

flowers are all fragrant, and there is a choice of single and fully double blooms. They are not fussy plants and will continue to bloom even when somewhat neglected.

For climbing trees, the creamy-white 'Moonlight' is a good choice. Almost immune to disease, it is a real tearaway in a warm climate, and needs only some initial tying in of the canes to romp away into the top branches of tall trees. For a more compact plant with a strong fragrance, the charming double apricot blooms of 'Buff Beauty' have lots of admirers.

Polyanthas

Abundant small flowers in clusters are the hallmark of the Polyanthas. Many are compact plants, well suited to container growing, but others will send up long canes that arch attractively. Polyanthas repeat flower reliably

over a long season. Their parentage is uncertain, but they have long been popular, despite the fact that many have no fragrance, as they are showy, sturdy garden and container plants.

'The Fairy', one of the world's favourite roses, is a Polyantha hybrid and bears large trusses of mid pink blooms. It is well known for its generous blooming over a very long flowering season. Incredibly hardy, it seems to be always in flower, and can be left to its own devices to sprawl or may be trimmed to shape for growing in tubs or where harsh winters make hard pruning a necessity.

Ramblers

Most of the roses in this large class are once flowering, but this in no way detracts from their spectacular beauty in full bloom. They are best when allowed to spread and ramble at will, covering many metres, and they will form a shapely, abundant mass of flowers

'The Fairy' (Polyantha hybrid)

during the season. There is a wide colour range available, and many are fragrant. Some flower in spring and others in summer, making an even wider choice possible. Select specific cultivars according to the characteristics you want: once flowering or repeat flowering, single or double flowers, fragrance, colour, growth habit; ramblers can provide it all.

'Veilchenblau' is an eye-catching Rambler bearing clusters of richly scented, deep violet to lavender blooms with an occasional white streak. If you yearn for a white Rambler, then 'Sanders White' is floriferous and vigorous, bearing clusters of small, heavily fragrant white blooms.

If you are fortunate in having plenty of space at your disposal, plant some of the abundant and vigorous Ramblers and leave them to their own devices for a few years to best show off their grace and singular beauty.

Chapter 2

MODERN ROSES

'Just Joey' (Large-flowered)

LIKE the old-fashioned roses, modern roses come in several classes, and within each of these is a very wide selection of cultivars.

Large-flowered Roses (Hybrid Teas)
These are probably the most favoured of roses grown by today's gardeners, and are the result of crossing the Hybrid Perpetuals with Tea roses. The class was first introduced in the mid-nineteenth century and has been steadily popular since that time.

Hybrid Teas have long, tapered buds and the flowers, often borne singly, open to be large, shapely blooms, often with high centres. They repeat flower throughout the season, beginning in early to mid-spring, and sometimes continue in mild areas until they are pruned in winter. The plants are hardy and vigorous and many are fragrant. They last well as cut flowers, particularly if there are plenty of petals to hold the shape of the blooms. Each passing year sees a bewildering offering of new Large-flowered Roses on the market, some of which will fade away never to be heard of after that first year of introduction, while others make it onto the 'best seller' and 'most popular rose' lists for many years, becoming classics of their type.

'Peace/Madame A. Meilland' is probably the world's best known and loved of these roses. The huge, creamy-yellow flowers are tinged pink, and the plant can grow very large in temperate areas. For a perfectly shaped white, 'Pascali' may be the choice. If you yearn for something just a little different in Hybrid Teas, then the loosely formed apricot blooms of 'Just Joey' will enchant you. They billow open from slender buds and spill their glorious fragrance all around the garden.

Cluster-flowered Roses (Floribundas)
When it comes to popular roses for the home gardener, these may well be the best choice for a great show in the garden, producing a

'Friesia'/'Korresia' (Cluster-flowered)

Climbing roses

Modern Climbers, unlike most of their Rambler ancestors, are usually repeat flowering. They have generally thicker canes than the old-fashioned Climbers, and less of them, which makes it rather easier to train them in the desired manner. Many originated as mutations or 'sports' from bush roses of the Large-flowered or Cluster-flowered type. Some, however, have no bush form, and are only available as Climbers.

There is nothing quite like a Climber for giving a garden the appearance of permanence, whether that garden is large or small. Climbers take up no more ground space than bush roses and will drape themselves ornately over fences, arches and pillars. Given some support by tying in the canes, they will grow up and over high walls. Modern Climbers are more restrained in growth habit and less likely to 'run amok' than the Ramblers, hence they are more suitable for smaller gardens and town houses. Smaller-growing Climbers can also be grown in large containers to provide a feature on balconies and verandas.

Climbers give height to a garden, and can provide a background for other plants (especially more roses!). They are available in a wide array of colours, some with blooms borne singly, while others have blooms in clusters.

'Handel' is a top performer. Its creamy blooms edged with carmine and generous blooming habit endear it to everyone who grows it. It provides abundant flowers for picking while leaving enough on the plant for a great show in the garden. If you want a floriferous deep red Climber, then 'Dublin Bay' never fails to please with its rich colour and huge blooms.

Miniature roses/Patio roses

These wonderful little roses may be called by either name, depending on local convention. Often the larger-growing Miniatures are called

mass of colour, as the blooms are borne in clusters both large and small. They were first bred by crossing Hybrid Teas with Polyanthas, and it is from the latter class that these roses derive their cluster-flowering habit. From the Hybrid Teas, they inherited their shapely blooms. They repeat flower endlessly throughout the season and are constitutionally very strong, making them less liable to attack by fungal diseases. It is often hard to decide if a rose should be classed as Large-flowered or Cluster-flowered, as many seem to have the attributes of both, resulting in a blurring of definitions between the two classes.

Picking a sure-fire winner here is at best a risky business, but it's difficult to look past the glowing lemon-yellow blooms of 'Friesia', which are large, generously produced and fragrant (disproving the theory that you can't have everything; when we're talking roses, you can, and in so many ways). 'French Lace' stops me in my tracks every time, its pinkish-ivory buds unfurling slowly to rich cream blooms with exquisite fragrance. But the most arresting sight I have ever seen is a huge plant of 'Priscilla Burton' in full bloom; the great trusses of flowers splashed all over in pink and cerise. Unforgettable!

Above: 'French Lace' (Cluster-flowered)

Below: 'Dublin Bay' (Climber)

Patio Roses, and the same name is frequently given to Miniatures that are budded onto rootstock rather than being grown from cuttings, thus making them larger plants. In either case, the plants have small flowers and their foliage and growth habit are in proportion to the flowers.

Miniature Roses are repeat flowering, and were bred by crossing the Large-flowered Roses or Cluster-flowered Roses with Polyanthas, the former usually providing the flower shape, and the latter the dwarf growth habit.

Like larger roses, Miniatures may vary in size from the exquisite 'Si', with buds the size of grains of wheat, and not growing much over 8 cm, to much larger plants if given a gentle climate and good feeding and watering. There are climbing Miniatures too, some growing over 1m in good conditions, and these are the perfect choice for a small garden, patio or terrace.

These little roses can be fragrant too. The

'Wenlock' (English)

'Graham Thomas' (English)

creamy blooms of 'Little Scotch' are at the top of my list for incredible fragrance and shapely blooms. 'Minnie Pearl' is also a delight in creamy-pink. If, however, you want a deep red Miniature, 'Beauty Secret' is always reliable and the clear, bright yellow of 'Ko's Yellow' brightens any garden space.

English Roses

It's certainly difficult to place these roses in any of the above categories because they defy such classification. David Austin of Shropshire, England, has bred them, and he describes them as having "The form, character and growth of the Old roses, with the repeat-flowering habit and wider colour range of the modern roses. English roses are, in fact, repeat flowering Old roses."

Almost all of the English Roses are fragrant, and most are in soft, muted pastel tones. They were bred to be grown as shrubs, and they have a form and delicacy that certainly ties them to many of the old-fashioned roses that

Austin has used in his breeding programme. Leave them to grow so that their graceful growth habit can be appreciated.

I can't go past the wine red, fragrant blooms of 'Wenlock', a vigorous grower with truly opulent, fully double blooms. For a larger plant, 'Graham Thomas' is a spreading shrub that can be trained in the style of a climber or left to arch its canes in all directions. I prefer to let it lean gently on a fence for support. Its full, golden blooms are generous with their fragrance.

Whatever type of rose appeals to you, the choice of individual cultivars is a very personal thing, and you should make selections with your own garden in mind: whether it is rambling, small and formal, 'cottagey', or a terrace or patio garden.

But be warned that rose growing is highly addictive, and that breeders and nurserymen will offer new delights each year, entwining the gardener ever deeper under the spell of the rose; 'rose fever' is contagious and thankfully has no cure!

Chapter 3

THE NEEDS OF ROSES

'Proud Titania' (English)

THERE is no secret to growing good roses. However, much mystique seems to have grown up around the subject, sometimes making rose growing sound extremely difficult and esoteric. It is simply a matter of understanding what roses need to flourish, and this involves a large portion of common sense mixed with some specific information about how to provide optimum growing conditions. If the basic rules are followed, it is within every gardener's capabilities to grow wonderful roses with very little fuss.

Sun

Roses need sunshine and plenty of it. This is perhaps the only rule on which all rose growers will agree. Everything else, drainage, good air circulation, absence of competition, shelter, soil, water and food, can be 'arranged' by the gardener except sunshine. The first and most critical task is therefore to select the sunniest site for your roses as is possible. The minimum requirement is probably 5 hours per day, and anything over that is a bonus. Roses grown in full sun are less susceptible to disease and will bloom better and for longer than roses eking out an existence in the shade.

Air circulation

This is another vital aspect of rose growing. The plants must have air freely circulating around and through them and this will prove to be a boon in warm, humid climates where the risk of fungal infection is high. For this reason, avoid planting against solid walls and fences or any structure that will restrict air circulation. In addition, growing roses too close together can foster the spread of disease, so close planting should also be discouraged.

Absence of competition

Roses are hungry, greedy plants and do not like having to compete for nutrients with large trees or shrubs which are also hungry plants. Large trees have roots extending underground at least as far out as their branches, the feeder roots being in the region of the drip line at the edge of the foliage. If you want to plant roses to climb trees, then be sure to plant them well *inside* this drip line, where they can be assured of adequate nutrients. You can supplement their feeding for a few years without the tree's feeder roots grabbing all the food.

In general, it is better that roses do not have to compete with large trees and shrubs, but variety in beds can be achieved with annuals, bulbs and perennials. If you can match the feeding requirements of such companion plants with the needs of the roses, so much the better.

Companion planting

This is a widely used practice which involves growing compatible plants in close proximity to each other for the mutual benefit of both. In the lists that follow, specific plants have been included because they enjoy the same situation and feeding as roses, and bestow benefits of one kind or another while the roses, in turn, give to the companion plants their own singular beauty. Some of the benefits of companion planting may be merely aesthetic. Combining other plants with roses gives a more established look and adds luxuriance and abundance to the beds and the garden in general.

Shrubs

Some winter and early spring-flowering shrubs can be planted to soften the bare look of winter-pruned roses. These might include forsythias, viburnums and some of the smaller growing magnolia varieties such as 'Stellata', a variety with starry white flowers in early spring.

Perennials and annuals

Some obvious choices from an aesthetic point of view are all the lavenders (*Lavandula*), which enjoy sun as much as roses, and add their own special fragrance to the garden; rosemary (*Rosmarinus officinalis*) is another choice for the same reason and you can choose from the upright or the prostrate forms. Both lavender and rosemary have foliage that forms an attractive contrast to the roses.

Suitable varieties of perennials and annuals will form a low-growing carpet of plants under the roses, thus forming a natural 'living mulch', which will retain moisture in the beds by reducing evapo-transpiration, prevent wide fluctuations of soil temperature and suppress weed growth. Choose plants that need no maintenance themselves, and you will quickly and easily improve the appearance of garden beds.

Some suggested plants are:

Alyssum maritimum (Sweet Alice) An annual of generous self-seeding habit that generally bears white flowers, although pinks and apricots are available. Masses of flowers rapidly smother the ground. Excellent when combined with *Lobelia inflata* (see below) for a soft carpet of colour that readily suppresses weed growth.

Chamaemelum nobile (syn.*Anthemis nobilis*) (Chamomile) Low-growing, mossy foliage with a rich fragrance when crushed. Delicate white flowers, or in the case of the variety 'Treneague' no flowers, just the fragrant foliage, which releases its fragrance when crushed.

Anthriscus sylvestris (Queen Anne's lace) a tall grower with fern-like foliage and a mass of tiny white flowers in large umbrels. Hardly a ground cover, but wonderful behind and amongst the roses for its massed effect. A perennial or biennial which will self-seed.

Campanula (Bellflowers) These perennials are available in many colours. They will readily self-seed, and taller, 'pickable' varieties blend well with roses, while shorter ones

Mass planting of 'Sylvia' (Large-flowered)

make a charming ground cover.

Cerastium tomentosum (Snow-in-summer) A perennial with silver-grey foliage and white flowers. It is ground-hugging and stem-rooting in habit, spreading quickly to form a blanket of white across the ground. The variety *C. columnae* is less rampant than others.

Dianthus (Pinks) These are low-growing plants that flower profusely in colours from white through pinks to maroon and are often heavily scented. The old white cultivar 'Miss Sinkins' is hard to beat for reliability and fragrance. Clumping in habit, *Dianthus* can be divided to form new plants.

Gypsophila (Baby's breath) is one of those 'naturals' for combining with roses, in the vase as well as in the garden. Annual and perennial varieties are available in pinks as well as white. The foliage is fine and delicate and the flowers are small and starry, appear-ing on long, pickable stems.

Lobelia inflata (Lobelia) A low-growing annual in blues, pinks and white. Tiny flowers are delicate, and the plants will spread, trail and self-seed in most situations.

Nepeta mussinii (Catmint) Hazy, grey-green foliage and tall spikes of lavender-blue flowers. Best when planted *en masse*.

Nigella (Love-in-a-mist) Annual with pink, white, blue or plum-coloured flowers, which are wonderful when massed closely together to form a misty mass of colour. Self-seeds readily.

Thymus (Thyme) There are many varieties of this low-growing and fragrant perennial herb. The foliage is intensely aromatic, and the specific aroma depends on the variety chosen. Thymes spill their foliage and tiny flowers over the edges of garden beds and pots. They are hardy, low-growing and spreading in habit.

Violas (Violets) These are always a delight

with roses, and many are self-seeding, ensuring a continuity of new plants. Most are deliciously fragrant and will spread to form large clumps, which should then be divided and replanted. If spider mite is a problem in your rose garden, violets may well be the host plants, so watch for signs of the pest in hot, dry weather. Pansies, of the same family as violets, are always reliable as cheery ground-cover plants throughout much of the year and, like violets, many will self-seed. *Viola tricolor,* known as 'Johnny Jump Up' or 'Heartsease', is a joy, constantly renewing itself by seeding and appearing in odd corners everywhere in the garden.

Bulbs, rhizomes and corms

Many of these can be planted amongst the roses and left to naturalise, forming clumps that need not be disturbed unless the flowering begins to fail. It is best not to select those varieties that need lifting each year, as this disturbs the roots of roses and may result in unwanted sucker growth. Also avoid, if possible, those that have unsightly foliage after the flowering period, although such foliage may be gathered up and knotted to retain a neater appearance, while still allowing it to die down naturally as it should. Some suggestions are crocus, hyacinth, narcissus, bluebells, day lilies and many of the iris species.

Companion plants that will benefit roses

These can be conveniently divided into two groups: plants that benefit roses through their abilities to fix essential elements in the soil and plants that have insect repellant or attractant qualities. Leguminous plants have the ability to fix nitrogen in the soil, in nodules on their roots. Blue lupins are often planted as a green crop in new garden soil, then dug in before flowering, thus releasing the nitrogen for the plants that follow. More decorative lupin varieties can be grown amongst the roses as companion plants, ensuring a contin-

'Scabrosa' (Rugosa)

uing supply of that most crucial of elements, nitrogen. Sweet peas, besides having this same effect, look and smell wonderful on climbing frames as a background for roses.

Borage, an annual herb, also stores potassium and calcium, thus ensuring a supply for your roses. Borage, flowering in blue or white, will self-seed readily and has the added benefit of attracting hoverflies, wonderful aphid predators, to a garden, as its dainty, nodding flowers come into bloom.

Comfrey is another plant that stores much needed elements in its parts; in this case, nitrogen, phosphates and large amounts of potassium. Comfrey, however, can get out of hand very quickly and develop into a forest while your back is turned so don't plant it in the same beds as the roses, but keep it within a defined boundary somewhere else in a corner of the garden and use the leaves as a mulch for the roses and in the compost heap. Potassium is of inestimable value to roses as a protectant against fungal disease.

An insect repellant plant that will keep unwanted underground pests from your roses is the marigold, which repels nematodes and eel worms from the roots of roses. *Calendula,* the Pot marigold is the best to use for this effect. Other insect repellant plants that could be included in rose plantings are pyrethrum (*Tanacetum coccineum*), which is a source of the natural insecticide of the same name. The plants are attractive, bearing small white daisy flowers which can be steeped in boiling water to produce your own insecticide spray. The plants are hardy and self-seed readily. Southernwood is a shrubby insect repellant, as is the bright yellow flowered tansy. Lavender repels most insects, hence its use in bags in linen and clothes cupboards. The herb marjoram also repels insects.

Garlic is problematical; I have never found it to repel any insect, though other gardeners disagree. I find that it attracts aphids in great numbers, and if the aphids are all massing on the garlic perhaps they will leave the roses alone. Many other benefits have traditionally been ascribed to garlic, but the ultimate answer is to try it for yourself, as a repellant or as an attractant, and if all else fails at least you can eat the produce!

Plants that *attract* predator insects can also be used to advantage in the rose garden. Predator insects like lacewings, praying mantises, ladybirds and hoverflies will all help to keep the insect pests under control without the gardener having to resort to potentially dangerous chemicals. So it is well worth growing some of these as companion plants, too, for the ecological balance they provide between predator and prey; the prey usually being aphids, which, despite our efforts, are never entirely eliminated from roses. You can reduce their numbers by growing honesty (*Lunarium*), an attractive shrub with its 'see-through' seed pods, and an attractant for ladybirds, lacewings and hoverflies. The blue flowers of *Phacelia tanacetifolium* also attract hoverflies, the larvae of which will decimate the aphid population. (Plant closely with roses for best effect.) All of the plants of the *Apiacea/Umbelliferae* family, which includes Queen Anne's lace (see above) and the herbs dill, angelica, coriander and parsley, are good

'Rosy Carpet' (Ground cover)

predator-insect attractants, and can be included with roses for this reason, as well as their pleasing appearance and numerous culinary and medicinal uses.

It is rare to find in nature any plant growing alone; plants grow together with other plants for one reason or another. It seems a pity, then, that many rose fanciers plant their roses apart from the rest of the garden in solitary splendour, then spray masses of chemicals on them to achieve the same effect that could have been achieved by judicious companion planting.

Drainage

Tolerant and adaptable plants though they are, roses will not survive long with their roots permanently in water. 'Wet feet' spells death to roses, as waterlogged soil cannot expel carbon dioxide and will become sour, as aerobic soil bacteria are not able to survive in such an environment.

A well-drained position is therefore essential. If this does not already exist in the place you have in mind for roses, then you can manipulate the site to suit via one of two possible alternatives. Firstly, you could consider installing a drainage system, and while rather arduous work for the average gardener, this may be essential if your mind is set on rose growing. Plastic drainage pipe is as effective as terracotta, and much less expensive. Keep in mind that the water you drain from the rose beds will inevitably end up somewhere else, so make provision for this in your plan. Consider the effect of a sudden, severe cloudburst that may lead to a spontaneous lake somewhere in your garden — an awe-inspiring and infuriating way to learn about drains!

If a drainage system is beyond your ability or pocket then the obvious choice is to raise the level of the rose beds above the level of surrounding areas. This can be done by first creating some sort of retaining wall to hold the weight of the extra soil you will be using. Concrete edging, a low rock wall, treated timber, railway sleepers and bricks can all provide the edging that is essential to hold the new bed together and to prevent the soil from washing away to the lowest level. Do, however, keep that sudden cloudburst in mind and make the retaining wall just a little higher than you anticipate you will need. If very large retaining walls are being built, such as on a steeply sloping site, the weight of soil contained by such walls will be considerable, so the structure must be built almost as far underground as it is to extend above ground.

Having constructed the retaining wall, you will then need to create a depth of around 30 cm of good topsoil. This can be done all in one hit by the purchase of topsoil (check that it is weed free), or by building up the level over a period of time with well-made compost, peat, grass clippings, manures of all kinds, seaweed, sawdust, pumice, sand (unless your soil is already sandy) and commercially prepared, bagged soil mixes from garden centres. Shredded newspaper will do very well too, as will fine to medium bark chips. Anything that will form humus (decomposed organic matter) in time is acceptable, and that includes all kinds of garden waste, although shredding and composting will

build up good soil faster. Aim to create as much topsoil as you can, even if the recommended 30 cm seems unattainable at first. You can of course keep adding material to the top of the beds for many years in the form of organic mulches and that will keep the humus content well up. Clay soils that are too water retentive can be broken up with the addition of gypsum, pumice or a commercial brand of clay breaker.

Try to add all this material to the beds some months in advance of the rose planting, so that it will have time to consolidate and be incorporated into the soil by weather and the action of earthworms and soil biota. There is no need to dig it in; just give nature half a chance and the work will be done for you. Keep the spade for digging holes for planting your roses.

Shelter

In very exposed places, roses will need shelter from prevailing winds. This is because if the plants, especially when newly planted, are exposed to strong winds, they will be rocked to and fro, tearing their roots all the time, thus weakening their grip in the soil. Strong prevailing winds could also affect humidity and evapotranspiration, and in coastal areas there is the additional problem of salt-laden winds. If you do garden in an exposed area, try to provide some kind of windbreak for the roses in the form of a trellis or a shelter belt of other plants that will break the force of the wind to which the roses are exposed. Certainly stake the roses firmly when you first plant them, and tie them in well. It may be necessary to provide taller, stronger stakes as the plants grow. Standard roses are particularly prone to wind damage and must always be secured with a stake to avoid the budded part, the scion, being completely torn from the rootstock.

Keep in mind the requirement for good air circulation and sunlight however, and don't

Standard rose

Bud union high on rootstock

A spectacular climbing rose.

build any solid structure too close to the plants, or attempt to close out all of the wind, as this will result in turbulence coming from all directions as the wind finds its way around solid objects.

Soil

If your soil grows other plants well, even a good assortment of weeds, then it will also grow roses well. It's that simple! Roses will grow in nearly all soil types, but few soils are so perfect that a little help from the gardener won't result in even better roses. Ideally, the soil should have plenty of humus and soil biota, and be crumbly textured. So when planning to grow roses, the better the quality of the soil you can produce, the better the roses will perform. The two important factors with soil are *condition,* that is, the structure of the soil, whether it is basically clay, loam,

sand and so forth, and *content,* that is, the nutrients the soil contains and their availability to the plants' roots. Both condition and content can be easily altered, so you can have absolutely any kind of soil at all and still grow roses to your heart's content. Any gardener, however inexperienced, can manipulate the soil to suit rose growing.

If at all possible, do all of your soil preparation well before planting. Several months before is ideal, and purists will do it possibly a year ahead of time, but don't let that put you off. Make your soil as good as you can given the time and materials at your disposal, and the roses will thrive, provided that you feed and water them abundantly.

Sand

Roses just love sand. One look at the brilliant roses growing in parts of coastal Western Australia would convince you of this fact. The difficulty is that sandy soil does not retain water or nutrients, so the structure of the soil must be improved to allow both of these essentials to be held in the soil for uptake by the roots. Incorporate as much organic matter as possible into sandy soils. Again this does not mean that you have to dig endlessly; just add the material in layers, with some blood and bone to help it break down, and the earthworms will do the rest with the help of the rain. Obviously, aged materials will break down and become part of the structure of the soil faster than new materials, but it depends how much of a hurry you are in and how accessible good, aged, well-mixed compost is to you. In the absence of such a mix, add anything you can lay your hands on that was once alive, and shred it first if you can, so that it decomposes more quickly. If you don't have a shredder, toss all the plant material down in front of the lawn mower and that will do a fair job of shredding for you, provided that you don't ask it to shred very thick materials which may well blunt the blades. Keep adding blood and bone, as the breakdown of organic matter will for a time use up nitrogen in the soil, and you need to replace that nitrogen for the roses to use. Once the condition of sandy soil is improved, the content is no longer an issue.

Peat

This soil type will grow excellent roses if some of the elements it lacks in its natural state can be provided. Treat with a good dressing of lime, and add to this some basic slag, the dross from iron works if it is available, as this not only contains iron, but also traces of calcium and other elements. Phosphates and potassium may also need to be added before planting too, so the addition of all kinds of organic matter as described for sandy soil will be beneficial. The difficulty with peat soils is that if they dry out completely, as they can and do in drought conditions, then it is extremely difficult to get the soil wet again as it becomes almost impenetrable by rain. So add humus-forming materials and try to keep adding organic mulches annually to help hold moisture in the soil.

Pumice

This is an improvement on pure sand, as it will retain water a little longer, but like sand, pumice requires a great deal of organic, humus-forming material to be added to it, along with phosphates and plenty of blood and bone for the breakdown process. Often missing from pumice soils is cobalt, an essential trace element, so a general proprietary rose food, which contains traces of cobalt as well as other trace elements, is advisable every year or two. But first improve the condition of the soil with humus, otherwise whatever you add in the form of extra nutrients will simply leach out. This is a clear case of needing to get the condition of the soil right before the content issue can be addressed. In most cases, once the condition of the soil is right, the content can be left to sort itself out with just the regular addition of well-made compost and manure. However, with plenty of water available, pumice soil will grow marvellous roses.

Clay

Clay soil retains water well (sometimes too well), but because the clay particles are bound so closely together, the water is not available to the roses' roots. This of course means that nutrients carried to the roots in water are also not easily available, and the plants could well struggle to stay alive. The compact clay particles also mean that the soil is poorly aerated. Fortunately, clay can be easily improved and it is one of the best possible soils for roses. The clay needs to be augmented with lots of organic matter in the same way and with the same materials as sand, peat or pumice. Apply liberal dressings of these materials whenever possible, prefer-

Opposite: 'Remember Me' (Large-flowered)

ably aged and shredded, and dress with gypsum (calcium sulphate) to render the clay more friable and thus easier to work. This is another case of getting the condition right first and the content improving as a result. Various proprietary clay breakers can be purchased, and these are usually composed of peat and fine bark, with some compost and dolomite. They do a splendid job in breaking up clay soil. If you are keen to dig the material in, by all means do so, but digging is not essential as the rain and worms will aerate and mix the organic matter if left for a few months. Remember that if your soil is of the clay type, then good drainage is crucial!

Chalk

Roses do very well in chalk soils, which by nature are usually alkaline. If surface topsoil is shallow, add some bagged soil and plenty of composted material as a mulch to help the soil to retain water. Chalky soils are always 'hungry', so build up the humus levels and keep the mulch layer topped up. This will also help to neutralise the alkalinity to a certain extent. Aged fowl manure is an excellent addition to the compost. Roses grown in chalky soil will always have good depth of colour.

Cheating

If you are just unable to bear the prospect of waiting months before planting a rose or two, then cheat! Buy a bag of good soil or tree and shrub mix, dig a very large hole, and plant each rose in the mix. Add a thick mulch of compost, which can also be bought if you like, and water in very, very deeply. This will sustain the roses perfectly well, and they will reward you with wonderful blooms during the flowering season, motivating you to prepare more beds to grow the endless lists of cultivars that you are sure to compile once 'rose fever' gets a hold.

The pH content of soils

All soils are either acidic, alkaline or neutral, and the degree of acidity or alkalinity is measured by the pH scale, which registers a figure from 0 to 14, with a neutral reading at 7. Numbers lower than 7 indicate an acid soil, and higher numbers an alkaline soil. But this doesn't mean that you have to rush out and have soil tests done, and it certainly doesn't mean that a calculator and complicated mathematics are necessary to ensure the right level for your roses. If roses were that fussy, then nobody in their right mind would grow them, and they would certainly never have survived in the wild for so many millions of years.

Roses are really very obliging when it comes to pH levels, and will grow well anywhere between about pH 6.0 to around pH 8.5, and that's a huge range. Lots of people get quite twitchy about this and insist that roses must have an acid soil, but that is simply not the case; if it were, then roses would be difficult to grow in the mostly alkaline soils of Barcelona, and certainly would not grow near the Murray River in Australia. The fact is that roses do very well in these districts, and can positively flourish in slightly alkaline soils.

There really is little need to consider acidity or alkalinity except to understand that heavy feeding and organic mulching will over time increase the acidity of the soil, so you may need to counteract the acidity with an annual dressing of dolomite or lime in early winter. Use dolomite for preference as it contains the trace element magnesium, often deficient in coastal areas. The magnesium in the dolomite will be made available to the roses by the action of the acidic soil itself. Obviously, super alkaline soil will be made more acidic by the addition of organic materials such as compost and mulches. Don't resort to adding artificial fertilisers to your soil unless you know precisely what you are about, as an oversupply of one element may decrease the availability of another and you will end up on a chemical addition and subtraction roundabout, never actually growing

Mass plantings of roses give impact.

anything but obsessed with soil chemistry; and that's not the idea at all!

Ongoing feeding

All plants need feeding on a regular basis, and roses are no exception to this. You can feed them exclusively with a well-mixed compost without ever having to use any artificial fertiliser; that is how roses were sustained for millions of years before they were cultivated as garden plants. However, artificial fertilisers are certainly very handy, as they provide a balance of nutrients required by roses in the correct ratios and they are easy to apply.

The roses won't know the difference, provided they are fed adequately. But the soil biota will, and if plants are fed on an unremitting diet of artificial fertilisers the soil biota die. When that happens, the soil is not able to sustain plant life at all, let alone roses, because its structure breaks down completely and no organic matter can be incorporated

into the soil if the living organisms in that soil have died. Healthy soil produces healthy plants! So use mainly organic fertilisers in the form of animal manures mixed with vegetable matter, composted well, and you will be certain that you are doing the very best for the soil and, as a result, the roses. Most garden centres stock a variety of animal manures and composts if you have no direct access to them, so supply these to the roses on a regular basis and nutrient deficiencies simply will not occur in your garden.

As a general principle, feed roses lightly when they begin active growth in late winter or early spring, depending on local climate, and again in mid-spring when the first flush of blooms is ending. The next feeding can be given in late spring to promote summer flowering. In warmer climates, such as southern Africa, South America and the southern parts of the United States and England as well as India, Australia and New Zealand, a magnificent autumn blooming can be obtained from repeat flowering cultivars if they are fed heavily in mid-summer and lightly again in early autumn (see Chapter 8).

NPK content

All fertilisers contain various nutrients, but the three most important nutrients for roses are nitrogen, phosphorus and potassium. The percentage content of various fertilisers is expressed by the NPK ratio. N stands for nitrogen, P for phosphorus, and K for potassium. This is printed on packets of commercial fertilisers, which will give the ratio expressed as NPK 8:4:10, or something similar, depending on the precise contents of the fertiliser. NPK 8:4:10 just happens to be the perfect balance for roses. But natural fertilisers, manures and composts have measurable NPK too, although it may not be printed on the bag. Fowl manure is the closest to ideal for roses, with cow manure coming in a good second. Horse manure and sheep pellets are good too, so if you can vary the food occasionally you will be sure that the roses have all they need in the way of a balanced diet.

Trace elements

Besides this 'big three' of elements, plants need many other minor elements in minute quantities. These are called trace elements, and will be present in most soils anyway, and certainly supplied in sufficient quantities if you use well-mixed compost on its own or in combination with manure.

For the record, the most important trace elements needed are calcium, present in blood and bone; magnesium, contained in dolomite and fish meal; sulphur, contained in almost all composts; iron, contained in blood and bone; boron, contained in fish meal and soot, as well as in powdered borax, which also contains some calcium; manganese, contained in animal manures; and zinc, copper and molybdenum, also contained in animal wastes.

Compost

So the essential ingredients of a good compost are animal manures, vegetable matter, blood and bone, and some fish meal if you can include this. Try to add organic matter from other sources besides your own garden to ensure that there will be no deficiencies. The compost can be made on site in bins or heaps, but what matters is that the materials in the brew are varied, added in layers and left for long enough to be well incorporated into a crumbly, sweet-smelling mixture before being used in the garden.

Keep the bottom of the heap or bin on the soil so that earthworms can get in and do their valuable aeration and mixing, and add their castings which have a high nutrient value, and there will be no need for the laborious process of turning the compost. Just leave it for a sufficient time to decompose, then spread it straight onto the beds as a mulch. Extra ingredients can be sawdust, kitchen refuse, lawn clippings (although they are perhaps better left on the lawn to feed

itself), dead flowers, tea leaves, wood shavings, seaweed (try to rinse most of the salt off first), garden weeds (except persistent weeds like oxalis), shredded newspaper, and anything else that will break down over time. Layer the materials and supplement with blood and bone and lime occasionally. Use this brew and you'll never have to even think about condition and content, pH balance or NPK ratios.

Liquid feeding

The feeding of roses with dilute forms of liquid manure can be a useful booster to the health of the plants. When sprayed on, the leaves take up nutrients from the water, and the nutrients are then translocated to all parts of the plant. But it is very easy to err on the side of generosity with these liquid preparations and end up burning the leaves, especially if the product is sprayed onto leaves in warm, sunny weather. Always use the preparations exactly as indicated in the directions for a particular product or make them up a little on the weak side to be absolutely safe. This is one case where more is definitely not better. More can in fact be lethal, and there is no substitute for reading directions on containers and using common sense. Liquid fertilisers can of course just be watered onto the soil in the rose beds.

Water

Without water, there is no point in fertilisers or manures of any kind, as it is water that carries the nutrients to the roses' roots in an available form. Water must always be liberally applied before and after feeding or mulching, and during the growth period, and roses more than most plants appreciate long, deep waterings on a regular basis. An absent-minded spray with a hose on warm summer evenings will not do; it is in fact worse than useless as it encourages the roots to grow into the top few centimetres of soil where they can easily be burned on the next hot day.

Roses create an effective display in public gardens.

Water deeply on a far less frequent basis, and the roses will send their roots deep into the soil where they will find moisture and suffer no harm. Watering will always be more important than feeding, but don't go overboard and water so deeply that the food you have applied is all washed away. Try to water early in the day to allow the foliage to dry before nightfall, thus minimising the risk of fungal diseases, and adjust your watering regime to your own type of soil and climate requirements. If you are able to choose and install a watering system, a trickle system is the best possible choice, as far less is lost through evaporation, and the foliage is not wet for long periods. But, however you do it, make waterings generous rather than often, and apply a mulch before summer, keeping it topped up through the season until autumn; it can then be left over winter to become incorporated into the soil by earthworms and provide humus which will help retain moisture for the following season.

There are many low-growing, compact plants that can be grown under roses as a 'living mulch'. These will have similar moisture-retention qualities to other mulches, and will help keep the garden weed free. As a bonus they are attractive and take away the bare soil look. Alyssum, chamomile, lobelia, thyme and violas all fit the bill nicely, and also add their fragrance to the garden. (See Chapter 3).

Chapter 4

BUYING AND PLANTING ROSES

'Duc de Cambridge' (Damask)

IF you are a methodical gardener, you will have decided on the kind of roses that you want to grow, prepared your beds well with regard to site, drainage, air circulation and soil (and earned my undying admiration!), and then you will be ready for buying your plants. Some guidance may be needed as to what constitutes a good plant and how to plant it so that it grows well in your garden.

Roses can be purchased as Standards, most of which have been budded on about 1 m from the ground, giving the effect of a rose 'tree', with no lower branches at all. This type of rose is wonderful for a formal look in the garden and is often used to advantage in lining driveways and walkways in larger gardens. Standards can also be used to good effect when grown in containers on verandahs, terraces and patios, or anywhere that ground space is at a premium. Some popular rose cultivars are routinely budded on as Standards by nurseries (that is, the buds of the

desired cultivar are grown on suitable rootstock), and many growers will bud on a specific cultivar as a Standard 'to order'. Standard roses should have had two buds inserted into the rootstock in order to have bushy, vigorous top growth. Look for plants that have growth all around the bud union (where the bud has been budded on to the rootstock).

It is possible to obtain Miniature roses as standards, usually with a shorter rootstock more in keeping with the miniature type of rose that is budded. Most growers also offer weeping standards, which have a trailing type of rose budded on so that when well grown the branches will droop gracefully in the same manner as weeping cherries or willows.

The most popular method of budding roses is as bushes, and this involves inserting the bud from the desired cultivar, the 'scion', low on the plant, in most cases just a few centimetres from the ground. The great majority of roses are budded on in this manner, and it

'The Fairy' grown as a standard.

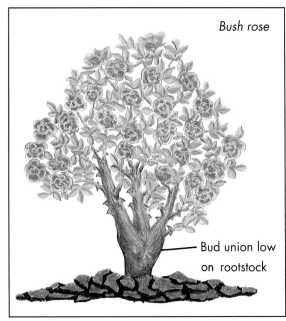

Bush rose

Bud union low on rootstock

is preferable if the bud union is close to the ground, as this makes a more stable plant, less liable to rock about in the wind and break, as can sometimes happen if bush roses are budded with a long shank between ground level and the bud union.

Bare-root roses

You can select your plants from the catalogues of rose nurseries and have them sent to you in the winter as 'bare-root' plants, or purchase them in this way from retailers. The term 'bare root' means that there will be no soil with the plants; just the rooted plant packed in probably a plastic bag with damp newspaper, sawdust or sphagnum moss around the roots to keep them moist.

If you are buying bare-root plants, which are sold only in winter to very early spring, there are some points to look for to ascertain

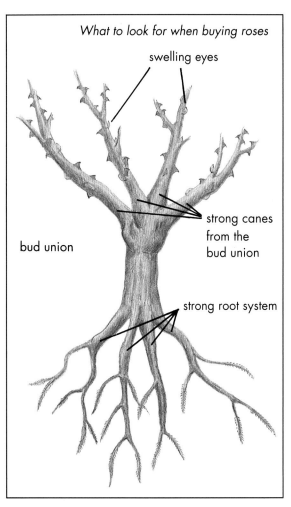

What to look for when buying roses

swelling eyes

strong canes from the bud union

bud union

strong root system

that you have a first-class plant. Firstly, there should be at least three good, strong-looking canes, preferably evenly spaced around the bud union, and you should see growth eyes along these canes. The canes will probably be green, but may also be brownish depending on cultivars and the age of the plants. Some of the growth eyes may have started to shoot and that is a sign that all is well. When selecting your plants at a nursery or garden centre, reject completely any that have only spindly canes, less than, say, a pencil thickness, as these will take a much longer time to establish in the garden. Most plants offered for sale will be two or three years old, hence the strong canes that are visible.

It does not matter in the least which way the growth buds are facing, despite the fact that many people go out of their way to find a plant with buds growing outwards. After you get the plant home is the time to decide which way you want the new canes to grow; it may well suit your purpose to have the new growth facing inwards, to balance the bush, or to avoid the new growth sticking out across a pathway or heading straight into a fence. The amount of foliage is irrelevant as this will vary according to what time of year the bushes are lifted from the nursery ground and to some extent will reflect the mildness or severity of the preceding winter.

You may not be able to see the roots if they are packed in a lot of damp packing material, but you need to know what you are buying, so establish with the retailer that the plants have a strong, balanced root system, and that the roots have not all been chopped off to be fitted easily into the plastic bag. This can happen sometimes, with roots trimmed to just a few centimetres, and that makes it very much longer before the plant will be able to get on with producing top growth, as it must establish a root system first. Growers are very careful with their stock and want to present only reliable plants, but the problem some-

When purchasing roses, look for strong canes.

times arises when the roses are packed for transportation. Some plants will have most of the roots growing only on one side, but this is immaterial; the rose is still perfectly sound and growth will most likely appear from the other side in the next season or two.

Container-grown roses

These are available at all times of the year, grown as the name suggests in containers, which are often polythene growing bags. The roses are growing in soil, probably with some slow-release fertiliser added so that they will grow and flower in their containers for a season. These plants may be purchased and planted at any time of the year with confidence, as they will almost certainly have a good root mass, which is what makes the foliage flourish.

Again, there should be at least three thick canes, with plenty of growth eyes. If possible, select those with canes spread evenly around the bud union, but having said that, there are some roses that don't get to that stage for several years, so don't reject a plant just because all the canes are on one side; new canes will appear over time from the bud union. Reject roses with only spindly canes and short, twiggy growth.

The roots of these plants will not be visible, and it isn't reasonable that you upend all the containers to look for a good root mass. (In fact it's a sure way of being thrown unceremoniously out of a garden centre!) But if you should find when planting a container-grown rose that all the roots have been chopped off short in order to fit the container, you have every right to return the plant and request a substitute.

Both growers and retailers want to sell good quality plants that will please the customer and ensure his return for further purchases, so every effort will be made to present plants in good condition. Some countries have standards by which rose plants are graded to ensure that the customers get fair value, a top quality plant when top price is paid. But in many countries, no such standards exist, so the customer needs to check that what he or she is buying is what is wanted: a strong plant that will establish quickly and grow well.

Planting bare-root roses

Bare-root roses should only be available in winter or very early spring; hence, that is the time they should be planted. When the parcel of roses arrives by mail order, or when you bring home your bare-root plants from the retailer, do not open the packages until the precise time that you want to plant them. If the roots are exposed to the air for even a short time, they will dry out and the plant may well die. So place the parcel of plants, wrapping and all, into a large container of water in a cool place to await the moment of planting.

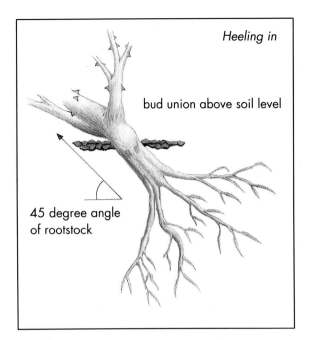

Heeling in

bud union above soil level

45 degree angle of rootstock

Heeling in

This may be necessary if you are not able to plant the roses within the next few days, and the technique will ensure that the roses remain in good condition, even for many months, if it is not convenient for one reason or another to put them into their permanent places. If this is so, dig a shallow trench anywhere in the garden and lie the plants down a few centimetres apart along one side of the trench at an angle of about $45°$. Cover the roots well and water them in thoroughly, treading gently to exclude any air spaces around the roots. Take care when heeling in to keep the plant labels visible for when you want to plant them out properly. The plants will remain in good condition provided that the soil remains moist, and heeling in is an excellent alternative if the beds are not ready when the roses arrive, if the soil is too wet to work, if you are planning to move house, or if you simply cannot attend to the planting for some time.

Permanent planting

Again, leave the plants in their packaging in a container of water until the moment of

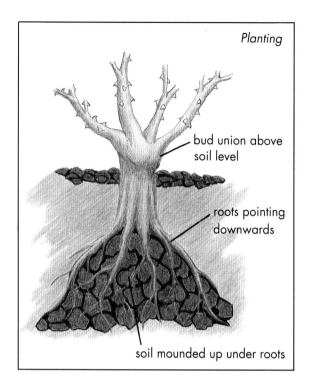

Planting

bud union above
soil level

roots pointing
downwards

soil mounded up under roots

top of this with the bud union just above the surrounding soil level. Note that in climates with severe winters, it may be necessary to have the bud union under the soil level so that it is not killed by severe frosts and snow cover. But above ground planting in mild climates means that suckers from below the bud union will be more easily seen and removed, and it also allows for later mulching without burying the bud union.

Settle the plant on top of the mound using some fine, new soil if yours is very heavy, and spread the roots out as evenly as possible, making sure that they are all pointing downwards. This is important, as upward pointing roots may produce suckers and these sap energy from the plant. Fill in around the roots with the fine mix, and keep filling until the plant is able to support itself. Gently tread the soil down and water in very thoroughly to avoid air pockets around the roots. Fill now to soil level, tread in again and water once more to settle the soil firmly around the whole area. Keep the soil moist for a few weeks to allow the roots to establish themselves properly. *Do not* add any fertiliser or manure at this stage, as it can burn fragile new root systems, but a handful of bone dust mixed in with the soil will assist root growth, and a light feeding of blood and bone or a compost mulch may be added to the surface after planting.

When planting standard roses, have the soil level at the same place it was before the rose was lifted from the nursery bed; this will be visible as a mark on the rootstock.

If it is necessary to stake newly planted roses, then drive the stake in before you plant the rose to avoid damaging the roots. It is always necessary to stake standards, and these should be secured using a single tie of a material that will rot in time, thus avoiding the tie cutting into the canes if it is overlooked for a time. Stakes can generally be made from bamboo canes or wood, but some

planting. This will ensure that they are in the best possible condition. Draw up a planting plan to keep, with the name of each rose in its appointed place, as, with the best of intentions, labels can often disappear from the garden. Mark out the places, allowing for sufficient space between plants. This is generally about 60 cm to 1 m apart for bush roses, with some allowances made for vigorous growers; standards need to be about 1-2 m apart, depending on what you plan to have growing around them; and climbing roses need about 2-3 m between plants, again allowing for the vigour of the selected cultivar. Space miniatures around 20 cm apart.

Having marked the positions, have a quick look at the size of the root mass of each plant as you come to it, as this indicates the size of the hole you need to dig (put the plant back in the water after you have looked at it). Then dig the hole large enough to enable you to spread the roots out and down without any crushing or damage. If any roots are broken, trim them off with secateurs. Build a mound in the hole so that the roots can be placed on

'Loving Memory' (Large-flowered)

people prefer metal stakes; the only precaution to be taken here is that the metal may become very hot in summer and should not actually touch the plant. Use only one tie on a standard rose, positioned right at the top of the understock and tied firmly. Ties lower down can cause the plant to bend over in strong wind and the stem may very well break off at the tie.

If you are planting climbing roses, remember to leave at least 30 cm between the plant and its intended support. This will allow you to keep that area free of weeds without tearing your arms chasing weeds under low-growing canes. It is as well to tie down all the canes on a climbing rose, if they are long enough, to ensure that the canes are heading in the direction you want them to grow. However, this is not possible when the canes are very short on new plants, so if this is the case, leave them for several months, tied in an upright position to secure them against the wind, and tie them down later. Climbers may not bloom in the first year, expending all their energy on producing new canes, so don't worry if that happens; wait until the second year and you will have flowers in abundance.

Planting of container-grown roses

These are available throughout the year in bags or pots ready for planting, and you can safely plant them at any time; however, avoid planting in very hot weather or the hottest part of the day. Give the plant a good soaking with water for a day or two prior to planting, to make sure that the roots are thoroughly moistened.

Dig the hole, judging the size the same as you would for a bare-root plant, but probably having to allow for a bigger root mass. Cut the container from the plant; don't pull the plant from the container. If the roots are a tangled mass, you will need to separate them from the potting mix in which they have been growing, as this will by now be drained of nutrients, so tap most of the soil away, or if necessary, hose it away. Place the plant in the hole with the bud union at the same level as it was in the container, except if you need to adjust that for a different climate (see bare-root roses) and spread the roots out carefully. Fill in with good soil as before and tread in gently, following with a very thorough watering; as much as the soil will take. Do not apply fertilisers until the next season, but you can always sprinkle a little blood and bone on top of the soil prior to watering in. Mulching is helpful in warm or dry weather to retain soil moisture.

Planting cutting-grown roses

Some nurserymen will give you a choice of budded roses on understock or cutting-grown roses, often called 'own root' roses. This means that they are not budded onto under-stock, but are grown in the nursery as cuttings, then grown on until they reach saleable size. The advantage of cutting-grown roses is that they will never produce suckers, and some roses undoubtedly thrive best when grown by this method.

The big advantage of budded roses is that the plants will probably grow bigger, and may produce more and larger flowers than they would do if grown on their own roots. If the budding process is used, nurserymen can get more plants from the same amount of bud-wood than they would if the same material was used for cuttings. It takes only one growth eye (or bud) for budding a rose, while several are needed to produce a good cutting-grown plant.

Miniature roses are commonly grown from cuttings, and nurserymen will explain in their catalogues which roses are cutting-grown and which are budded, with the latter often being more expensive to buy because of the skill needed in budding, and the fact that the plants are not usually ready for sale for two or three years.

'Friesia' (Cluster-flowered)

When planting cutting-grown roses, the directions above can be used, with the exception being that there is no bud union, so the depth of planting is not critical. Usually the best depth is that at which the rose was growing prior to lifting, and this will again be seen as a mark low on the stem.

Replacing roses

If a garden has been established for some years, roses may be removed for a variety of reasons and new roses purchased to take their place. An old plant may be past its useful life, or the gardener may want a change of colour or size, or simply want to try a new cultivar. In all of these cases, if it is possible to remove the old rose some months prior to planting the new one, so much the better.

But sometimes replacing a rose may be an 'impulse' decision, made at the moment a new cultivar is spied at a retailer's shop. Either way, there is a precaution to be taken. New roses *will not thrive* if placed in the same soil in which another rose was growing. The reason for this is not completely certain, and may be that the soil has become impoverished over a period of time, or it may be that the older rose has produced substances from its roots that kill the roots of the new rose by causing a temporary micro-organism imbalance in the soil. Whichever of these is true, the fact is that the new rose will not survive unless the soil in which the old rose was growing is removed and replaced with soil in which roses have not been grown. This can be new soil purchased in bags or soil taken from another part of the garden. The soil you remove can safely be placed elsewhere in the garden, or even scattered on the surface of rose beds.

It is usual to remove about a barrow load of soil from the hole, being sure to remove as many root fragments as possible. If replacing a rose that you have grown in a container, discard all of the soil in that container and replace it with fresh soil.

Keep in mind that the roses you are planting now may be in their positions for over 20 years, so it is worthwhile taking as much time as necessary to do the job properly in the first place, paying careful attention to soil, planting depth, watering and staking. Roses are long-lived plants and their roots will penetrate deep into the soil for anchorage and to search for the nutrients they need, so it is up to the gardener to provide optimum conditions for new plants.

Roses are not usually pruned before leaving the growers, but may have been trimmed for ease of transportation, so it may be necessary to trim new plants as they are received. I prefer to trim off any broken pieces at planting time, and then later to go over the plants again, pruning to a good growth eye in the direction in which I want the growth to face (see Chapter 6). The main point is to make your cut above a live bud; its direction is your choice. When planting container-grown roses at times other than winter and early spring, trimming is unnecessary, except to remove any broken pieces or any twiggy growths too small to bear flowers.

Whenever you plant roses, firm the soil in well and give them a few good soakings to help get them established. Mulch heavily if planting in summer or during hot weather; in the latter case it is advisable to defer planting, if possible, until conditions are cooler.

Chapter 5

PESTS AND DISEASES

'Vesper' (Cluster-flowered)

NOW that you have selected your plants and have them well planted, trimmed and watered in, and have a feeding programme underway, what else must you consider?

Many intending rose growers are put off by their perception of roses as being terribly prone to pests and diseases, yet this is not really the case at all. Roses are no more pest and disease prone than any other plants. The difference lies in our image of the rose; we expect it to be perfect in every way, and so we are more likely to notice imperfections in the form of a diseased leaf or a slightly mis-shapen bloom. We are conditioned to accept nothing less than perfection in rose blooms, and this is where the perception of roses as being pest and disease prone begins. Do we expect absolutely faultless snapdragons, or lavender, or any other plant in the garden? No, we don't, but unreasonably we expect roses to be without any visible imperfection. Perhaps we need to have a change of 'mind

set' in order to accept roses as they are, not as we have been led to think they should be.

Certainly roses will be attacked by pests. Certainly there are diseases that affect roses, but no more or less than will affect, say, carrots or geraniums, so why demand that roses be without what are, at worst, minor inconveniences? It's a case perhaps of not being able to see the wood for the trees; in looking so hard for signs of pests and diseases, do we forget to see the roses?

Insect and other pests

If roses are grown together without any sort of interplanting with other species, they will certainly be more likely to be attacked by specific pests. Monoculture is, at best, a very risky business and positively invites pest infestations on roses as well as food and other crops. A far better approach is to grow your roses as part of your garden's total ecosystem, paying due regard to botanical diversity, which is Nature's way of maintaining a balance between plants, animals and insects. If there is nothing else for the odd insect pest to eat, then of course it will eat the roses! If, however, there are other, tastier things to eat, the insects may well leave the roses alone. Other plants will provide homes for predatory insects like ladybirds, hoverflies and praying mantises, all of which will happily dine on whatever pest is eating the roses.

Thus, the first line of prevention against pests is diversity in planting. The second line of resistance is to keep the roses growing strongly, with a varied diet and plenty of organic, natural food. Keeping the soil healthy will keep the roses healthy, so keep in mind that what is good for earthworms and other soil biota is also good for roses.

Let's be realistic and accept that we are not going to totally eliminate insect pests without serious misuse of chemicals. At best, we can control infestations to minimise damage. Apart from predatory insects, small birds will play a large part in keeping insect pests to a minimum. But if you start using the 'quick fix' method of wholesale slaughter with insecticide sprays, then you will only find that specific insects become 'problems' and increasingly harder to control.

Insecticides are generally not specific in what they kill; they will kill all insects, the bad, the good and the indifferent, so when you reach for an insecticide spray, you are wiping out the very means of natural control of whatever pest you are trying to eliminate. Clearly when birds come to eat the sprayed insect pests, then they too become part of the poisoned food chain that is created. Rachel Carson explained this chain reaction in her book *Silent Spring* many years ago, but we still seem loath to heed her warning as it applies to all of us as gardeners. Consider for a moment that 90% of the product you spray does not hit the target. Where then does it go? The Arctic ice contains pesticides, as do most of the soils, rivers, seas and lakes on Earth,

and it is indiscriminate use of chemicals that is doing this irreversible damage to the environment as well as being a causative factor in many human diseases.

Alternatives? Of course! If you plant insect-repelling plants along with your roses, they will help keep insects away from the roses (see Chapter 3, Companion planting).

The predatory mite *Phytoseilus persimilis* is a voracious predator of the two-spotted mite, or spider mite, and will happily keep this pest under control for you if it has somewhere to live in the garden. But once you start on chemical insecticides of one sort of another, then you have undone all the good that your interplanting has done. Other plants, provided they don't grow too large or are not too greedy, will enhance the garden and the health of roses by providing homes and food for beneficial insects.

No matter how well we watch and protect our roses, there are some pests that will occur from time to time, and one should be able to recognise the type of damage they cause so that preventive action may be taken.

Sucking insects

This group includes aphids, which cluster on new rose buds and foliage and are often green, but sometimes red, brown or yellow. They suck the plant sap, sometimes to the stage where the buds are unable to open. Aphids breed at a truly phenomenal rate, so any action you take against them will have to be repeated frequently during the season. For the stoic, aphids can just be squashed between thumb and forefinger. They can also be simply hosed off with a good, strong jet from the hose, and predator insects will do a great job, aided and abetted by small birds. If aphids are really getting you down, you can spray them with a natural pyrethrum spray which kills on contact. Aphids are pesky, but will not become a problem if you are often about amongst the roses and dispose of the first cycle that hatches in spring. Overfeeding

Aphids cluster on new growth.

with nitrogenous materials results in excessive vegetation growth high in sugars, which is an open invitation to aphids.

Scale insects are also sap suckers, and may be noticed at pruning time. The insects appear as waxy, white spots, usually on older wood. The waxy coating is in fact the outer, waterproof coating for the colonies of insects which live on sheltered parts of the canes. If badly affected, growth may be stunted. As the outer coating is waterproof, a horticultural oil is needed to break through that covering and suffocate the insects underneath. Spread the oil, diluted at the recommended rate, with a toothbrush or sprayer over just the affected areas and a couple of days later go back with a brush and scratch the scales off. Repeat applications may be needed if the outbreak is severe.

Some mites are sap suckers too, and are not insects but arachnids. Nevertheless they come under the broad heading of sap-sucking pests. The European two-spotted mite, or red spider mite, is the one that causes damage to roses, mainly on the foliage, and the mites responsible are very small, barely visible to the naked eye. Their presence is indicated by fine thread-like cobwebs on the undersides of leaves, or by the reddish mass of myriads of mites together. The leaves may be dry looking, discoloured and pale, sometimes faintly brownish-yellow between the veins. Spider mites can overwinter in many common garden plants and weeds. Fortunately the predatory mite *Phytoseilus persimilis* is an avid eater of these mites and can be introduced into the garden to control this pest, without recourse to miticides. These predators can often be purchased by mail order if they are not already living in your garden. If this or another predator mite is not available, then a miticide made with fatty acids or potassium salts may be used. Spider mites tend to prefer hot, dry weather, so keeping the roses well watered and occasionally spraying the undersides of the foliage during hot weather will help to deter them.

Chewing insects

Beetles, weevils, katydids and caterpillars form the bulk of these pests, and fortunately they are larger and more visible to the naked eye than the sap suckers, and so may be more easily noticed and removed by hand. The presence of chewing insects is indicated by holes in the leaves, often about the edges, or chewed young growth and buds, so if you see this sort of damage look for the insect that is the cause and remove as many as possible by hand. You may prefer to use a natural pyrethrum-based spray, quite organic, but effective as a contact insecticide. Spray only the insect pests though, and don't take a 'blitzkrieg' approach, as that will also kill beneficial insects like bees and predators. Caterpillars tend to lurk on the undersides of leaves or roll themselves up in leaves, and some beetles only feed at night, so you may need to make some evening forays during the growing season to catch them in the act.

Rasping insects

These creatures scratch at the surface of leaves so that they can then suck the sap from

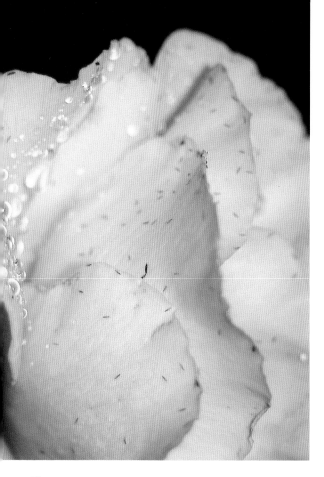

Thrips may appear in spring.

them. Most are capable of flight, and will rise up from disturbed foliage. Thrips (tiny, winged, black insects that move in hordes), while not usually a great problem to roses, come into this category. They may arrive in spring and attack the edges of petals, sometimes so badly that the flowers cannot open and simply 'ball' and rot on the stems. Foliage badly affected by thrips will have a silvery appearance on the leaf surfaces. Whitefly move in hordes too and can be suspected if the leaves are yellowish. Rasping insects appear in all shapes and sizes, depending on climate and location, but look for the tell-tale sign of pale, silvered foliage.

All rasping insects can be killed by the use of horticultural oil sprayed onto the leaves, and a natural insecticide like pyrethrum may be added for a better kill rate if your roses are really badly affected. But it is far better to remove by hand the pests you can see, and if necessary spray only visible pests. Don't use oils in hot conditions; pyrethrum is a better choice under these circumstances.

Soil pests

The most common of these are nematodes or eel worms, small worms that are parasitic on plant roots. Pot Marigolds (*Calendula officinalis*) are often grown as companion plants with roses to deter these pests.

Galls

Are rough growths that may occur on the roots of roses. These are the work of soil-dwelling organisms, but poor drainage fosters such growths. Roses so affected should be destroyed, and the surrounding soil removed too.

Diseases

Those rose growers who live in climates with a harsh winter have an easier time with regard to diseases than those who garden in warm and temperate climates. Even though diseases may attack the roses, they are unlikely to linger in and on the soil over severe winters to emerge again in spring to wreak havoc for yet another season. Very cold winters are a bonus when it comes to prevention, as any left over spores will be killed by the cold.

Diseases on roses can be minimised with good cultural practices: planting roses far enough apart so that the foliage of one doesn't touch the next, ensuring there is free and unimpeded air circulation around and through the plants; and collecting up and burning any fallen leaves which may harbour diseases. Strongly growing roses, with plenty of organic food, are far less likely to fall prey to disease than roses short on a balanced nutrient supply.

There are other ways too of minimising disease outbreaks in your roses. Always choose the early morning for overhead watering, so that the foliage has a chance to dry before nightfall. This will limit the spread of fungal diseases like blackspot, rust and mildews which can only proliferate in a humid environment.

When selecting roses for your garden, choose those cultivars recommended as being the most disease resistant in your area. Local gardeners are the best source of information of this nature. Local rose nurseries also often give information about the disease resistance of specific cultivars with their descriptions in catalogues. The Rugosas are the most disease-resistant class of roses I know of, being completely untroubled by fungal diseases.

If you have a choice of watering systems in your garden, the best type from a disease prevention point of view is a drip or trickle system, which will water the root area of the plants without wetting the foliage. Obviously this is also the best choice from a water conservation point of view, as less moisture will be lost through evapotranspiration. Another management technique that can be employed in disease prevention in humid areas is to use only short-growing plants amongst roses. Avoid thick plantings of tall-growing plants close to roses, as this will restrict air circulation, increasing the humidity around the plants, and thus encouraging fungal diseases to spread. Breeders are well aware of the desirability of 'disease proof' roses, and you can be certain that disease resistance is a trait that all breeders want in their roses. So keep an eye out for rose trial ground reports on new cultivars, as these give a good indication of which roses do particularly well in your local climate and soil conditions.

In warm and temperate climates, it is usual to give roses one or two 'clean up' sprays with lime sulphur during late autumn and early winter. This is an essential part of the overall hygiene of the rose beds, killing any lingering fungal spores while the plants are dormant over winter. (Don't spray the soil surrounding each plant, as the sprays are toxic to earthworms.) During this same period, it is also recommended that the gardener spray twice with copper and oil, usually with at least 2-3 weeks between the copper and oil and the lime sulphur sprays, as the two are incompatible. Both lime sulphur and copper are accepted in organic gardening, but neither should be overdone, and we need to keep in mind that the picking up and burning of all infected foliage is essential. When selecting a copper spray, bear in mind that cupric hydroxide is preferable to copper oxychloride, as the latter contains chlorine, which is definitely not accepted organically. When using these and any other chemicals in the garden, mix and use the products only as directed on the containers, and be aware that lime sulphur will stain woodwork, including painted surfaces, so keep the spray drift well away from such areas. Lime sulphur also smells diabolical, so try to select a day when the neighbours are out! As a consolation for the awful smell, remember that the product is disposing of spider mites as well as disease spores.

Black spot

The symptoms of this common disease, as the name suggests, initially consist of black spots on the leaf surface. The spots may be circled by yellow, and badly infected leaves will fall prematurely. Serious infections may quickly cause defoliation, reducing the ability of the plant to photosynthesise. If you notice any infected leaves, remove them at once from the plant or ground and burn them; they should never be incorporated into the compost heap, as the fungus will flourish under these conditions, and will be reintroduced into your garden with the compost. Spores are carried by wind and by contact, and can also be splashed from the soil up onto lower leaves by water. Cut back a badly affected plant at any time of the year to prevent the disease from spreading.

Rust

Rust is a serious fungal disease that can

Black spot can cause defoliation.

Rust appears first on the underside of leaves.

spread rapidly if not noticed and controlled at an early stage of infection. It tends to occur during hot, wet weather. Small, orange pustules appear on the underside of the leaves, and the spores, like those of black spot, can fall to the ground and be splashed back onto the plants via watering. Treat as for black spot by removing and burning affected parts of plants and by mulching. Sometimes rust will appear one year and then not be seen again. There is no doubt that some rose cultivars are particularly susceptible to rust, and are more so in humid climates. Extra potassium provides resistance to fungal diseases.

Powdery mildew

This disease first appears as a fine, white dusting over the shoots, young leaves and buds, which may become distorted if left unchecked. It may occur where air circulation is inadequate, such as under the eaves of houses where climbing roses are sometimes

grown, and often appears during hot weather, when the nights are cooler. Remove affected parts of the plants, trimming quite hard if necessary. One method of control is to use a solution of baking soda. Use a teaspoonful to 2 litres of water and add a commercial spray 'fixer' to help the mixture adhere to the foliage. Some growers add a dash of milk or dishwashing detergent to their sprays for this fixative purpose. Powdery mildew is almost waterproof, so you may have to resort to two applications. Allow the first to dry, then hose it off and apply the second, this time leaving the spray on the foliage.

Downy mildew

This is recognised by purplish-brown patches on the leaves, and may also cause defoliation if an attack is left unchecked. It is often seen in spring, and can prevent buds from opening. Treat affected plants as for black spot and rust.

Powdery mildew thrives in sheltered areas.

Downy mildew may appear in spring.

Another fungal disease to watch for is damping off, where, in the case of seedlings, the whole plant collapses at the roots. This problem is caused by the fungi phytophthora and pythium. To prevent this, ensure there is free circulation of fresh air.

Fungicides

There are many of these available under various trade names and all are effective to a degree, but they must be used with discretion if used at all. The diseases may well be kept at bay, but at what cost environmentally? Some fungicides contain chemicals that are toxic to fish, birds, crustaceans, earthworms, amphibians and invertebrates, and many also contain chemicals that are suspected of being neurotoxins and carcinogens, as well as allergens and mutagens. It is far better in the long term to rely on good nutrition, good cultural practices and disease-resistant cultivars than

to climb aboard the chemical roundabout without knowing the long-term effects.

Liquid seaweed fertiliser, when used in a dilute solution as a foliar spray, can be extremely effective against fungal diseases. It contains potassium and manganese, and is rich in trace elements, thus giving an extra boost to the feeding programme. A cupric hydroxide solution can be sprayed on foliage at intervals to prevent fungal diseases.

Bizarre as it may sound, many organically minded rose growers use yoghurt in a very dilute form as a foliar spray to protect against fungal diseases. It's the same principle as the one we use when planting ground covers; we want the ground covers to make it impossible for weeds to grow, and that's what happens with yoghurt sprays. The foliage becomes populated with the harmless bacteria from the yoghurt, making it impossible for the fungal spores to get a foothold.

Bacterial diseases

The major one is known as dieback. It occurs from the top of the cane, causing the cane to brown off and die, often from a cut too far above a live bud at pruning time. Some cultivars are prone to dieback, and are better discarded in favour of those with stronger constitutions.

Viruses

Rose mosaic, as the name suggests, causes a mosaic-type pattern of cream-coloured lines to appear on some of the leaves. **Petal fleck virus** is rather more insidious, as its effects are much harder to discern. Plants with this virus will often show only a generalised failure to thrive, but in darker coloured blooms small, fine lines like veins may be seen on the petals, running towards the edges. **Rose wilt** may occur early in spring and cause the stems and young buds to wilt. Lower leaves may turn yellow with red markings and a whole shoot may die.

There is no cure for viral diseases, and as the viruses may be spread by a variety of vectors, including aphids, the plants should be removed and burned or otherwise disposed of as quickly as possible.

Plants with rose mosaic virus are best destroyed.

Hopefully, further non-toxic methods of disease control will continue to be developed, and gardening magazines are a good source of such information. Use natural methods of pest and disease control as often as possible instead of resorting to chemical warfare, but bear in mind that to be truly effective any method will need to be used on a regular basis, and there is no pest and disease prevention and control method quite as effective as regular wanderings by the gardener among the roses!

Chapter 6

PRUNING

'Lavender Dream' (Shrub)

IF the very thought of pruning roses causes you to go into 'panic' mode, then it is probably best to sort out a few basics first.

The first consideration is that the primary objective of pruning roses is to produce more blooms and give the plant more vigour. There are some secondary objectives too, and these are to assist the plant to remain disease and pest free and keep it looking tidy. What happens if roses are never pruned? The plants will continue to bloom for years, albeit producing fewer and fewer, poorer quality flowers, and the plant will become rather straggly and tangled, but make no mistake, it will continue to flower!

But what if I chop away at the plant and don't prune it properly? The word 'properly' is not in the vocabulary of roses; don't tell the rose you're a rookie pruner and it will never know the difference. Roses *do not* die from inexperienced pruning! If roses were that easily killed off, they would certainly not have

existed for so long. Happily, they are very forgiving plants. You will not kill them, no matter what you do with the secateurs, so relax and make it your aim to understand the reasons for pruning; it then all becomes a matter of common sense and personal preference combined with your particular growing conditions. Roses will flower no matter what you do or don't do in the way of pruning.

Roses regenerate themselves by sending out new canes every year as older canes become less vigorous and produce fewer flowers of diminishing quality. By understanding this, you will realise that by cutting out old, unproductive canes, you allow more light and growing space for the new canes that produce the most flowers. Cutting out old canes helps rejuvenate the plant and forces it to redirect energy into producing new canes rather than maintaining old ones.

Any canes that are diseased should also be cut out, to prevent the spread of disease to other canes. Badly disease-affected canes will not recover, they will only eventually die. Canes that are deformed or damaged in any way also need to be pruned out as they will not straighten up; you can include in this category canes that are growing in a direction that you don't want, for example, growing across a pathway, or hampering your access to other plants.

To sum up these aspects of pruning: **cut out all '3D' canes,** that is, Dead, Diseased or Deformed, and cut them out at the very base, flush with the bud union. This is the first step for all types of roses.

Having completed this '3D' operation, removing unproductive canes, you can go on to the next step. This involves opening up the centre of the plant, eliminating canes that cross each other, crowd each other, provide places for pests and diseases to lurk, or block sunlight and the free flow of air through the plant. Look at the plant and decide which canes are doing these things, or look as though they might do them by next season, and cut them out cleanly at the base. At this stage of the operation, also remove any small, thin, twiggy growths that look incapable of supporting a flower; they only serve to crowd the plant and divert nourishment away from the flowers. To sum up this section: **clear the centre of the plant.**

By now the plant will be looking much better and you will be able to see where you are going. It would be wonderful if the plant now looked somewhat like an open vase shape, but the fact is it may well look lopsided and silly. Never mind that, just go on to the next step, which is to shorten the remaining canes. When shortening them, make your final cut a few millimetres above a live bud eye. If you grow any of the old-fashioned roses, the shortening of the canes will be a very small part of the operation, and may well depend on your own personal requirements. You may want as much length as possible to cover a bank or wall, hence you need only nip off the

A standard rose after pruning.

extreme ends of the canes; however, you may want to cut the plant back very hard for one reason or another, in which case go right ahead. For some of the very old classes of roses, a very hard pruning in winter may mean no flowers for one season, but the flowers will come again, you can count on it!

If in doubt about whether to prune an old-fashioned rose, leave it alone for a year or two and see what happens. However, most modern roses are repeat flowering, and these benefit from shortening the canes by about one-third to two-thirds of their length in temperate climates. Where winters are very severe, it may be necessary to cut all the canes almost down to the bud union and mound up soil or other material around them to keep the plant alive through prolonged periods of frost and snow, but these are the only circumstances under which such hard pruning becomes necessary.

There are many rose growers who practise

hard pruning, cutting the canes down very low, and just as many who advocate very light pruning, allowing the plants to get quite tall and wide. This is all very much personal choice, and everyone prunes roses to suit themselves in one way or another.

To sum up the last part of the process: **shorten the remaining canes** to suit your own requirements.

So these are the three processes of pruning:
1. Cut out 3D wood.
2. Clear the centre.
3. Shorten remaining canes to suit yourself.

Tools

To put this pruning theory into practice, some tools are needed.

Secateurs should be the best you can find, and if cleaned after use and wiped over with oil, they will last for many years. They will need sharpening from time to time, and this is best done by a professional. Don't use your rose secateurs on thick tree and shrub branches, which will surely wreck the blades; save them for the job they were designed to do.

Some gardeners prefer to disinfect their secateurs after each plant is pruned to avoid transferring disease from one plant to another, but unless you are pruning plants with viruses, this seems unnecessary.

If your roses have been growing for a few years or are large plants, you may need a pruning saw or loppers to prune thick canes that secateurs will not cut. Loppers are virtually long-handled secateurs, and with these it is possible to gain much more leverage than with secateurs. Saws come in all shapes and sizes, some with curved blades that allow access to difficult parts of the plant. Try handling a few in shops to see what feels comfortable for you. Whatever you buy, make sure that sharpening is carried out routinely so that the tools don't cause damage to the roses by dragging at the canes rather than cutting.

Gloves are essential when pruning, so invest in a pair with leather on the backs. It is far more common to get scratches on the backs of your hands when reaching through a bush than it is to get scratches on the palms or inside the hands. Remember also that thorns will go straight through ordinary fabric into your fingertips, so leather fingers in gloves are a bonus.

Protective clothing is advisable for the task, and this includes shoes with solid soles and a long sleeved shirt to protect you from thorns, either on the plant or inadvertently stepped on while engaged in the exercise.

Take with you a large receptacle for the rubbish, and drop all the pieces in as you go to avoid having to pick them up later.

Pruning paste can be used on cuts to prevent the entry of disease into new cuts, but the same effect is gained by spraying with copper and oil after pruning has been completed. *Do not* use oil after summer pruning as leaf burn may occur.

Timing

In most cases, the main pruning is done in mid-winter, when the roses are at their most dormant. In climates with hard winters, timing will depend on the likelihood of frost killing any subsequent new growth.

In temperate and warm climates, pruning may be carried out at any time from mid-winter, and depending on the air and soil temperature, new growth will begin to come away shortly after.

On older plants, a wire brush can be used around the bud union to remove old bark and debris that may prevent new basal shoots from emerging.

Old-fashioned roses

Once-flowering varieties should be pruned after flowering has finished for the season. Just follow the three steps outlined earlier, cutting out '3D' wood, clearing the centre and shortening the canes, although less shorten-

After pruning, new reddish growth emerges.

ing is usually necessary than with modern roses. The Species roses, Gallicas, Damasks, Teas, Albas, Centifolias, Mosses, Portlands and Ramblers are all pruned by simply following these three steps. Cut out any very old canes flush at the bud union, so that new canes being produced will not be crowded. Remember that it is always the newer canes that will provide the best-quality flowers. The same procedure is used for the Bourbons, Boursalts, Rugosas and Hybrid Musks, and in these classes, shorten remaining canes to about one-third to one-half of their length if it suits your purpose. Hybrid Perpetuals are treated in the same way, but shorten remaining canes to suit your requirements, depending on whether you are pegging down the long canes or prefer to grow these roses as bush types; in the latter case, the canes will need slightly harder pruning.

Always bear in mind that these are *your* roses, so how you prune them is entirely your choice.

Modern bush roses

The same pruning method applies whether the roses are Large-flowered, Cluster-flowered, Miniature or Patio types. Follow the three steps above, and the decision on how short to cut remaining canes is up to you. Most gardeners in temperate climates shorten the canes to about one-half to one-third of their length, depending on the specific cultivar, whether it is a small or large grower, and the shape that the gardener has in mind. Remember that when removing an old cane, cut it flush with the bud union so that no ugly stubs remain and there are no handy niches for insects and diseases to lurk.

When shortening canes, always make your final cut a few millimetres above a live bud. In most cases, you will want the new growth to point outwards to avoid canes crossing in the centre and rubbing as they do when the centre is crowded. Select a bud facing in the direction you have decided on, and angle your cut to match the angle that the bud is growing. This simply allows water to flow away from the bud or growth eye so that it won't rot. Sometimes nature seems to conspire to defeat you, and the bud selected may not shoot at all, but you will notice that later in spring, and you can recut to a lower bud that is shooting.

Modern climbing roses

These are pruned in precisely the same manner using the three basic steps and removing older canes, but after pruning, the remaining canes need to be gently pulled down to near the horizontal, encouraging the plant to produce flowers from lateral growths along the whole length of the canes. If canes on Climbers are left to grow vertically on a permanent basis, they may only produce flowers at the tips. Try to train the canes into a fan shape, each year removing the old canes at the bottom of the fan, and lowering the rest one at a time, so that the newest canes are

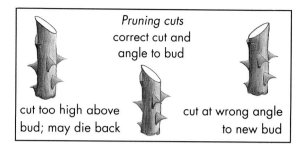

Pruning cuts
correct cut and
angle to bud

cut too high above
bud; may die back

cut at wrong angle
to new bud

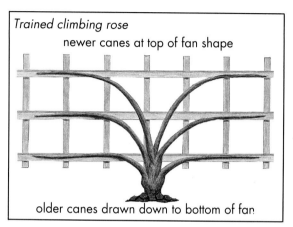

Trained climbing rose
newer canes at top of fan shape

older canes drawn down to bottom of fan

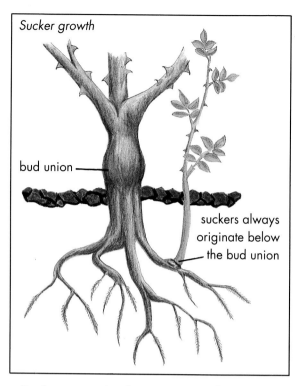

Sucker growth

bud union

suckers always
originate below
the bud union

always at the top. Tie canes firmly to their support, and use ties made of material that will not cut into the canes as they grow. Remember to check ties frequently and be prepared to renew them when necessary. Trim lateral growths from the main canes back to three or four good, strong-looking buds. If a cane refuses to bend the way you want, just bring it down as far as possible, tie it, then come back in a couple of weeks and lower it a little more until you've got it where you want it. Very strong canes can be softened and made more pliable by holding a container of very hot, steaming water underneath for a few minutes. Patience is required here, as if you force the cane, you may well end up with it in your hand and not connected to the rest of the plant... a humbling experience!

Suckers

With cultivars grown on rootstock, you may encounter the problem of suckers, shoots sent out by the rootstock. These need to be watched for and pruned out.

Sucker growth always comes from below the bud union, and will probably be a paler green than the foliage of the budded cultivar. It may have no thorns and will have no flower buds. If you see sucker growth, remove it at its source! If you just cut if off shorter, it will regrow with greater vigour and outgrow the budded cultivar, so find the source, which may be under the soil, and remove the sucker right at the base. However, don't confuse new basal shoots with suckers. New basal shoots, sometimes called water shoots, are the new canes being put out from the bud union and these should be staked and protected. New basal shoots are often pinkish and the leaves are larger than those on suckers.

Summer trimming

Many growers like to summer trim, or summer prune, their plants to give a spectacular autumn display. For a description of this technique see Chapter 8, Seasonal maintenance, under Mid summer.

Chapter 7

PROPAGATION

'Dainty Bess' (Large-flowered)

THERE are three methods by which roses are propagated. The first is by **cloning,** which involves reproducing an individual plant asexually so that all offspring are genetically identical to the original plant. This includes growing roses from cuttings, by layering and by tissue culture in a laboratory. The second method is by **budding** a growth eye from the required cultivar onto a rootstock; this is the most common form of propagation used by commercial rose growers. The third is by **sowing seeds** that have set and ripened in the rose hep.

Cloning
Cuttings
This is the method used most often by the home gardener. Cuttings are taken from a plant and allowed to grow roots, then the plants produced can be grown on in pots until they are large enough to be planted out into the garden. Some roses grow very easily

from cuttings and others are difficult to strike, but often success is determined by the medium used and the time of year that cuttings are taken.

The temperature will influence the time that cuttings take to root. Often good results can be obtained by taking cuttings from late summer and through autumn. At these times they will root readily, sometimes in 3-6 weeks if the cutting medium is right. Take cuttings from firm, current season's growth, preferably from a stem that has already borne a flower, the wood of which will be mature enough to strike roots. The cutting itself can be from a few centimetres to around 10 cm, but shorter cuttings will strike faster. Make the bottom cut straight across and just below a bud eye, which is the part of the cutting that will send out roots. Try to have several sets of buds on the cutting if you can, so that if one eye doesn't send down roots, then the next one might do so. Cut the top of the cutting on an

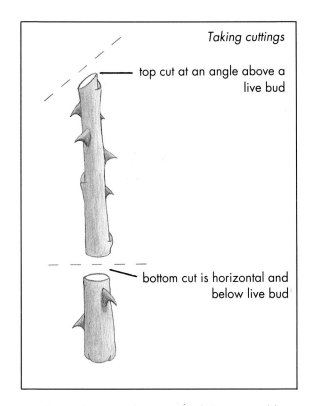

Taking cuttings

top cut at an angle above a live bud

bottom cut is horizontal and below live bud

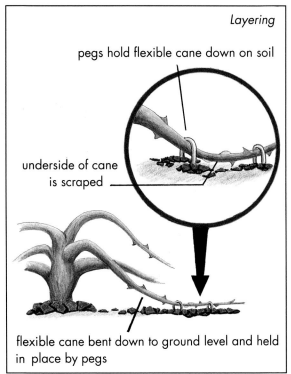

Layering

pegs hold flexible cane down on soil

underside of cane is scraped

flexible cane bent down to ground level and held in place by pegs

angle, so that you know which is top and bottom, and make the top cut just above a growth eye, as you would when pruning. Remove all of the leaves, or leave only the top ones, and plant the cutting very firmly about two-thirds of its length in the medium you are using. Pumice is an excellent medium for cuttings, as is perlite, vermiculite or very sandy soil. Do not feed the cuttings or put them into a rich mix. The cutting will produce roots in its search for food, and this is the reason for a 'no food' medium. Keep the cutting medium moist, but not wet, and if you can water daily that will help. Keep the pots outside preferably in semi-shade or dappled sun.

After 3-6 weeks, carefully turn the pot over and check to see if the roots are visible; if not, leave it for a few more weeks. When roots grow, they will be shiny-white to cream and easily broken. Carefully re-pot the rooted cuttings into standard potting mix, and keep potting up into larger pots with fresh mix until they attain sufficient size to plant into the garden. Cuttings don't mind being closely

packed prior to taking root; for example, you can put 100 tiny cuttings of miniature roses into a 1-litre ice-cream container and they will strike perfectly well. Growing cuttings is a no fuss way of increasing your rose collection.

Layering

This method is not often used, but can be a good method of propagating roses with long, pliable canes, like some of the Ramblers and Climbers. Select a part of a cane that is fairly straight, and flexible enough to bend to the ground. Scrape with a knife, along the underside of the cane, an area a few centimetres long beneath some growth eyes. Firmly peg this region with coat-hanger wire or something similar and secure it with a rock or two. It will help if you can fix it into some sand or pumice, or the same medium as you use for cuttings, as it must be free draining. Remove the leaves from the pegged section to the tip of the cane and keep the soil around the pegging moist for a month or two. When you can

Opposite: 'Old Master' (Cluster-flowered)

see new growth on this trimmed part, you can then carefully look for roots. When roots have developed, cut the rooted stem from the parent plant. Leave the new plant where it is for a month or two, but trim back the length of the cane to reduce stress on the root system. When a stronger root system has developed, the plant can be shifted to its final position in the garden.

Tissue culture

This is another method of propagating plants by cloning and, like cutting-grown or layer-grown plants, those produced by tissue culture are 'own root' roses, and will not produce suckers. They can, of course, be used to provide budwood for budding new plants, but in all ways they will be identical to the parent plant.

Tissue culture is carried out in laboratories equipped for the purpose and the method is being used increasingly to expand stock numbers for nurserymen, especially when the desired cultivar is only available in small numbers. Very little plant tissue is needed, and the parent plant is grown in controlled conditions in a sterile environment to keep microbe populations as low as possible. Tiny pieces of the plant are sterilised and placed on a gel into which is fed specific nutrients. When the 'explant', as it is then called, has developed a shoot, that shoot can be used to provide more explants or can be taken to the next step in the process which is the production of roots, accelerated by the use of auxins (rooting hormones). The plantlets are grown on and very gradually removed from their sterile, misty environment until they are ready to be grown outside.

Budding

In most cases, rose nurserymen use budding as their preferred method of propagation, and this is for two reasons. Firstly, many roses grow better if they are budded onto a strong rootstock. Secondly, for nurserymen who need to propagate many thousands of plants, budding is the most economical method; cuttings waste bud eyes, as several are used for each cutting. In contrast, budding needs only a single eye, so more plants can be propagated from the same amount of parent material.

Rootstock of a type suited to a particular area is grown from cuttings or from seed, and when it is the right size, buds from the required cultivar are placed under the bark of the growing rootstock and allowed to grow on until the plant is an appropriate size. Budded plants sold from nurseries are usually 2 or 3 years old, as it can take that long for the budded part, the scion, to attain sufficient size.

Budding is a very simple operation, and when you watch an experienced budder work it appears to be even more simple. However, it does take practice to become efficient at the job, and professional budders spend long hours bent over double under the summer sun. Most gardeners can bud for themselves at home if the basic technique is explained, and they have a little practice over a season or two.

Plants of the preferred rootstock are needed, and these can be grown in the manner described above for cuttings, except that when preparing cuttings of rootstock it is necessary to remove all growth eyes except the top ones to prevent later sucker growth from below the bud union. To make it easier on your back, these plants can be in pots so that you can do the budding on a bench or table. Different climatic regions will use a different rootstock suited to their growing conditions, so ascertain which is most suited to your own area and obtain some for your own use. Decide on the cultivar you want to propagate and make sure that the sap is flowing freely in both parent and understock, by watering well for a few days.

Summer is the usual time for budding, but start early, so that if your first attempts are

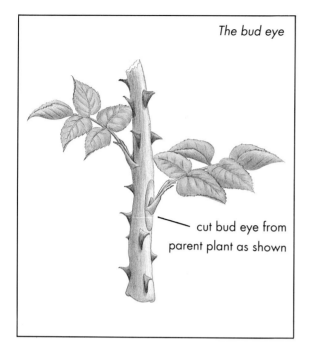

The bud eye

cut bud eye from
parent plant as shown

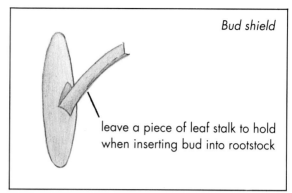

Bud shield

leave a piece of leaf stalk to hold
when inserting bud into rootstock

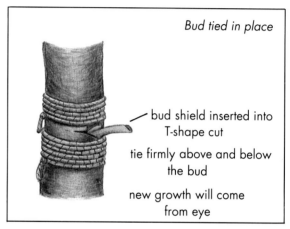

Bud tied in place

bud shield inserted into
T-shape cut

tie firmly above and below
the bud

new growth will come
from eye

unsuccessful there is still time for another try. You will need a sharp knife and some material for tying the bud in place; rubber strips used by nurserymen are good, but raffia will do, and so will soft plastic strips. To ensure that the budwood on the parent is ready, water it well, then try snapping a thorn off the wood. If it breaks off cleanly, the wood is ripe enough for the job. Cut yourself a few pieces of budwood about the same size as for cuttings, and make sure that there are some good, plump eyes on the wood.

Keep this budwood standing with the bottom in water until you are ready to use it and cut the leaves and thorns off to make the job easier for yourself. Make a shallow cut from about 2 cm above the eye to about 2 cm below the eye, and ensure that some of the cambium layer, the shiny layer just under the bark, is also removed. Aim to end up with a bud in the centre of a shield shape.

Make a T-shaped cut in the bark of the rootstock, fairly close to the root mass, certainly not more than about 8 cm above it, to ensure a stable plant. The horizontal part of the T needs to be about 3 cm long and the vertical part around 5 cm long. These should be shallow cuts that just slice into the bark and don't cut the cambium layer. Lift the flaps of the T shape with the end of your knife and slip the bud shield carefully and firmly into the incision so that most of the shield is in behind the flaps of bark. Trim the top of the shield to keep it flush with the rootstock. Tie the bud firmly in place so that the back of the shield is in contact with the cambium layer. Tie above and below, but not *over* the bud itself, and remember to attach a label with the name of the budded cultivar and the date. Keep the roots of the understock moist, but keep the budded area dry. If your bud has taken, this will be obvious in about three weeks, as the bud begins to swell. Soon after this, remove the ties to allow the bud to increase in size and send out a shoot. Then trim the top growth from the rootstock to divert nourishment to the new bud union. Keep newly budded plants protected from wind as the budding is still fragile and can be easily knocked off; stake if necessary. When new growth from the bud is about 10 cm long, trim off the top few centimetres to force the bud union to send out more shoots, all of which will make the union stronger. If possible, leave the budded plant where it is for a year; this will ensure a stronger union when the plant is set out into its permanent garden position. Budding is one of those operations that takes much longer to explain than to actually do, so if you are able to attend a budding demonstration you will see just how easy it really is, and probably gain the courage to try it for yourself.

Growing roses from seed

It is no more difficult to grow roses from seed than it is to grow poppies or carrots, so there is no reason why every gardener cannot grow roses this way. It's just a matter of collecting the ripened heps and sowing the enclosed seeds in the usual way. The trick, of course, is to select the best possible parents for the seeds so that the resultant seedlings are worth growing, and it has to be said that the chances of growing a really worthwhile new rose from seed are very remote. But don't let that put you off trying; all of the beautiful roses that we have now were once just seeds, and each year brings new roses onto the world market that were once just a gleam in a hybridiser's eye! It is by selecting the right parents that all of those brilliant new cultivars are grown to delight and enchant us. Selection of the right parents is the true art of the hybridiser!

Sowing a few randomly pollinated seeds first is probably a good idea, so that you get the hang of it before going to the trouble of selecting specific parents and trying for particular characteristics in the offspring. The wonderful thing about sowing rose seeds is that in most cases each seedling will differ from its siblings, and you are never quite sure what colour, shape or fragrance the new flow-

Many rugosas produce a bright display of heps.

ers will have. Waiting for your own first hybrid to flower is an amazing experience.

Any time from early summer is a good time to make a cross, as this will allow time for the hep carrying the seeds to ripen by winter. Some cultivars set heps readily, others set none at all, so you will need to choose a seed parent (mother) that sets heps easily. The pollen parent (father) can be any rose you like. The next step is to select a flower on the seed parent which is nearly ready to pollinate. When this flower is about two-thirds open, trim off all the petals except the outer ring, and very carefully cut off the stamens (which carry the pollen), in order to prevent self-pollination occurring. Take the stamens from the pollen parent and apply this pollen to the stigma of the seed-parent flower. You may see the stigma glistening, indicating that it is

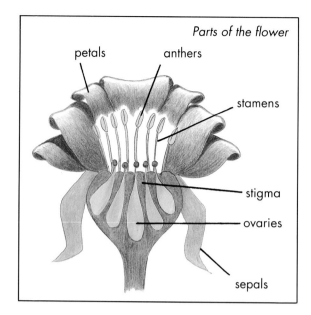

Parts of the flower

petals anthers

stamens

stigma

ovaries

sepals

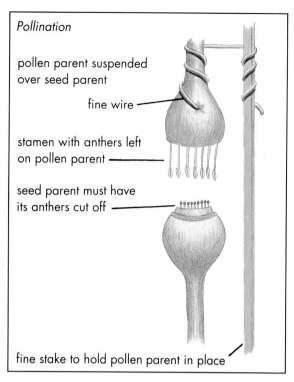

Pollination

pollen parent suspended over seed parent

fine wire

stamen with anthers left on pollen parent

seed parent must have its anthers cut off

fine stake to hold pollen parent in place

ready to be pollinated, but then again you may not, so do it anyway! Ripe pollen will fall from the anthers easily, so you can tell in this way if the pollen is ready. Pollen can be stored in a dry place for weeks, months, maybe longer, so if you want to be sure you've got ripe pollen when you need it, collect it prior to preparing the seed parent's flower. Test to see if it comes off easily on your fingers.

Alternatively you could tie the head of the pollen parent on a stake or wire above the prepared head of the seed parent and allow the pollen to fall when it's ready. All of this pre-supposes that no insects will sneak in and apply some other pollen of their own choosing, so after doing your pollinating, tie a paper bag over the head of the seed parent to prevent entry by pollen-carrying insects, and remove the bag after several days. Pollen can be applied by a moistened fingertip or a small paintbrush; the method doesn't matter a lot, just as long as you get ripe pollen onto a ripe stigma. Having made the cross, label the flower with the names of both parents, always listing the seed parent first. If successful, the hep will swell after a couple weeks. It is then just a matter of waiting for the hep to fully ripen, probably in late autumn or win-

ter, when you can harvest the heps for the next step.

Heps usually turn red or orange in autumn, indicating ripeness. Some will just shrivel and die, so make plenty of crosses so that you are sure of at least a few ripened heps with viable seed. If you live in an area with cold winters, the heps can be left to stratify out-of-doors, sitting on top of some sand in a pot and open to the weather. If winter isn't cold enough for the seeds to get a good chilling, remove the seeds from the heps after harvesting and put them in damp paper in a small plastic bag in the vegetable crisper of the refrigerator to stratify. Leave them until spring, when it is time to plant the seeds. If stratified outside, spring is the time to cut the seeds from the heps. Ensure that no flesh adheres to the seeds, as this can inhibit germination.

Sow the seeds in early spring about 25 mm deep and well apart in a container deep enough to allow for root growth. They can be indoors or out, whichever suits you best, but keep the seed-raising medium damp and allow plenty of light. Do keep the container protected from forays by snails, and put it somewhere so the cat can't select it as a personal sleeping place. Some seeds will germinate in just a few weeks, and others may take a year, so be patient, and pot seedlings up individually when they have four or more leaves. The first two leaves that appear will have no serrations, but the next two will be recognisable as rose leaves, so allow time for these 'real' leaves to appear. There is no rush in any of this, as the timing of rose tasks is never critical, and it is better to put off potting up for a while than to do it before the seedlings have decent root systems. Keep an eye on the seedlings for 'damping off' which can cause them to collapse suddenly at the base. Apply a weak cupric hydroxide solution to protect against this.

As they grow, feed them little and often, and gradually allow them more sun if you have grown them indoors. Keep the potting mix moist, grow them on in the sun and wait for the miracle of buds and then flowers on your own rose cultivars which you can name and keep if they appear to be good ones. The chances are most will be absolutely hopeless from a commercial point of view, but it's endless fun experimenting, and one day maybe you'll produce a world-beater. There is always room for another good rose on the market, especially if it is vigorous and healthy, has lots of flowers, good colour and is fragrant; all the qualities that we want in our roses!

Breeders worldwide go through this process multiplied by many thousands of times every year in order to obtain roses that they see as being commercially viable, and all of them aim for those same characteristics in their seedlings. In maybe less than 1% of the seedlings do they get what they are looking for, and that seedling is then budded on and sent to rose trial grounds to see how it performs. If it does well there, the breeder will patent it, name it and make it available to nurserymen so that the rose can be propagated in commercial quantities, possibly to become a world favourite in years to come.

Hybridising is a long shot, certainly, but it's a facet of rose growing that, like all aspects of this highly addictive form of gardening, can become obsessive, so be warned!

Chapter 8

SEASONAL MAINTENANCE

'Dundee Rambler' (Rambler)

ANY guide to the routine maintenance of roses needs to start at the point when new beds are being prepared. The timing of seasonal tasks for rose growers is not critical in any way, and can always be altered to suit the climate of individual areas and the gardener's convenience. In general, in areas with severe winters, tasks can be undertaken much later in the year than those same tasks would be done in warm and temperate areas. If in doubt as to the timing of specific tasks, local custom is often the best guide.

Prospective rose growers should be aware that the following seasonal advice is indicative only; it is by no means proscriptive, and is detailed here to indicate the usual times for cultural practices in the rose garden. Remember that roses grow and bloom because it is in their nature to do so. It is important to relax and enjoy roses; don't ever become so preoccupied with perceived maintenance that you forget why you grow them!

Mid autumn

This is the time to begin preparing beds for new roses to be planted in winter. Break up the soil in planned new beds as well as you can and include plenty of organic matter. You can dig this material into the soil if you like, but digging is by no means essential, as earthworms and rain will do the job of incorporating the organic matter into the soil. Do, however, give some consideration to the type of soil you have (see Chapter 3). Use plenty of decayed animal manure or blood and bone and lots of compost at this stage. You will only have this one chance to prepare the beds, and good preparation will pay dividends later.

In established gardens there will still be roses blooming, especially in warm and temperate areas, and the bushes may need to be protected against black spot, rust and the mildews. Keep an eye out for late aphids (see Chapter 5). If you are considering the purchase of a sprayer, get one much bigger than you think you will need, as rose gardens have a sneaky way of expanding to fill every space available! Keep the sprayer exclusively for rose sprays, never use it for herbicides, as it is easy for mistakes to occur.

Late autumn

Break up any clods still left in new beds. Be sure to remove all perennial weeds at this stage to save having to do battle with them once the roses are planted. In existing rose beds, collect and burn any diseased foliage, to prevent carrying disease over to the following season. Water the plants if lack of rain indicates a need for this. There should still be blooms being produced in warm to temperate districts. A mulch can be applied on existing beds, and by next season the material will have become incorporated into the soil to further improve its condition. Mulches are just spread on the soil surface and not worked into the beds.

Established plants can be given a thorough spraying now with cupric hydroxide and oil as part of the regular clean-up in the dormant months. If you have done some hybridising in the summer, then the heps may have ripened by now, so harvest them for later seed sowing (see Chapter 7). Cuttings of roses may still be taken at this time of year. In very cold districts, roses may now need a covering mound of soil or vegetable matter to protect them against freeze/thaw conditions that may occur in winter. If such conditions are likely, prune the roses very hard prior to mounding.

Early winter

If your new roses start to arrive from growers at this time of the year, they can be planted in permanent positions or heeled in according to your preference (see Chapter 4). Make sure any plants you are shifting are lifted and replanted soon; you may need to cut them back to facilitate digging them out, but leave the real pruning till later. Be sure to provide new soil if replacing a rose in the same position (see Chapter 4). Any plants that you have found to be badly affected by disease should be discarded. There is no point in persisting with roses that are not good 'doers' in your particular area, but it is recommended that a new rose be given three full years to reach its potential, so don't be too hasty to replace any in their first year or two.

It is time to spray existing roses with a 'clean-up' spray that causes them to drop remaining foliage, but if the roses are still blooming, this can be left until later in winter. Lime sulphur is the spray of choice here, to be followed 2-3 weeks later with copper and oil, and in warm and temperate climates it is advisable to fit in two sprays of each to be certain of eradicating all possible pests and diseases. However, be sure to leave the 2-week time period between the two sprays. Gather up all the fallen foliage and dispose of it carefully, don't place it on the compost heap.

Mid winter

Plant new roses as they arrive from nurserymen or appear at retailers, but if the soil is too wet or cold and the beds are not ready, the plants can be safely heeled in.

This is the main pruning time for most roses, but weather and your own inclination may change the actual time, so don't panic if you are a month late with the task as the timing is not critical. In warm or hot areas, pruning may be better left till a month later, so go along with local custom here. Prune your own roses; no-one cares about them like you do, and there is no better way to learn than by doing the job, which is really very simple (see Chapter 6).

Continue with the spraying of lime sulphur and copper and oil that you started last month; it will save a lot of bother with pests and diseases in the new season. If snow and ice are preventing you from getting into the garden, console yourself by reading about the

Above: Roses after winter pruning and *(below)* the same roses flowering mid spring.

diseases that you don't have to worry about!

Don't water or feed at this time. Check the ties on all of your plants to ensure that they are not too tight around the canes. In very warm areas, new growth may be starting to appear, so growers in such areas can enjoy the promise of spring at this early stage. There are pluses wherever you grow roses!

Late winter

If you did any budding onto rootstock in the summer, you can now cut the rootstock back hard and wait for new growth from the bud union in spring. All planting and pruning tasks should be completed this month as weather permits. Make sure you have collected all the prunings and any remaining fallen leaves to give your roses a clean start to the new season. Plants heeled in may be left until weather and soil conditions permit permanent planting.

Gardeners in warm and mild areas can feed their plants now, but others should wait until new growth is evident. Roses planted only this winter should not be fed at all. Once new foliage starts to appear, check to see if any bud eyes have failed to grow. If necessary, cut to a lower eye that is growing. Check the canes and rub out with your fingers any shoots growing into the centre of the plant, which will cause overcrowding if allowed to develop. Remember that good air circulation is essential if bushes are to remain disease free.

Seed can be sown now and into spring in a free-draining seed-raising mix. Keep the mix moist and wait for germination. The expectation of wonderful new cultivars of your own creation will give you something to think about besides the long days of winter.

If Climbers were cut back hard at pruning time, the canes can be re-tied now, preferably to the horizontal to allow for plenty of lateral growth which will produce the new season's flowers.

Early spring

If roses have been mounded up to protect them from a severe winter, do not uncover them until the danger of freeze/thaw conditions is over. Roses will withstand all but the harshest of winters, and light frosts will do little damage to the canes, but they may damage new leaf growth early in the season. If you didn't feed the plants last month, feed them now with a good compost or blood and bone with the addition of some rock phosphate, but avoid over-feeding with fertilisers high in nitrogen, as these will produce too much lush leaf growth at the expense of flowers, and invite insect pests.

A little potassium sulphate scattered on the beds and watered in at this time will help to keep the plants disease free. If any blind shoots form (canes missing the terminal flower buds), they should be cut back to the next five-leaflet leaf, and hopefully a new stem with flower buds will emerge from there. In warm areas there will be a few blooms from early-flowering cultivars; some of the Tea roses have this early-blooming tendency, as do some Ramblers and Species roses.

When new growth appears, keep an eye out for early aphids and destroy them when you see them. Humid areas may have some early black spot, so use the fungus preventative of your choice, taking careful note of the directions. Make the spray up as directed, but err on the weaker side at this time of year, as most sprays can damage young growth if made up too strongly or applied in the warmest part of the day. A weak spray of cupric hydroxide is safe and effective. Be sure to direct the spray up under the leaves.

Water deeply in the absence of spring rain, and be sure to water before and after applying fertiliser or manure to ensure that the nutrients get to the root zone where they are needed. Mulch can be applied now or next month, as the soil is warming up. Use organ-

R. nitida (species)

ic materials such as compost, sawdust, grass clippings or shredded newspaper so that the mulch can become part of the soil later on, improving its condition. A few handfuls of blood and bone can be used to prevent the mulch using up the nitrogen needed by the plants.

Keep cuttings moist and watch the newly emerging seedlings for signs of damping off. A few sneaky aphids will find the seedlings too, so keep an eye out for these. Don't despair if germination is erratic; that's just the way it is. Keep the seed trays moist and be patient. As seedlings grow, they can be pricked out and potted up as necessary. Any showing signs of weakness should be destroyed mercilessly; the world *does not* need any more disease-susceptible roses!

Top up the soil mix in containers, or replace about one-third to one-half, depending on how long the plants have been growing in them, and remember these potted roses in your feeding and mulching programme.

Mid spring

Plenty of new growth now, and flowering is well under way in warm districts. If your area is prone to spring winds, now is the time to stake and tie any new basal shoots that are very soft and may well snap in the wind. Water according to weather patterns, remembering that a long, deep watering once a week will always be preferable to light sprinklings every other day. Roses planted last winter can now be fed lightly, preferably with an organic material like blood and bone or a good compost, as artificial fertiliser may well burn the new roots.

When cutting blooms from new plants, cut only short stems at this time to avoid depriving the plants of nutrients stored in the leaves. Always cut just a few millimetres above a five-leaflet leaf. This is where a new shoot will emerge from the bud eye in the leaf axil and bear more flowers with repeat-blooming cultivars. This 'mini pruning' should be carried out all year, to ensure continuity of blooms.

Keep up the preventive spraying on a regular basis as a protective measure and keep at the aphids if the birds are not doing the job. Avoid the temptation to murder everything in sight with indiscriminate insecticide sprays. When spraying any material, apply only in the cool part of the day and never on windy days.

Watch that the mulch doesn't pack down too tightly, as it may then become almost waterproof. Grass clippings and sawdust have a tendency to do this, so if packing down is evident, loosen the mulch with a hoe, but keep the hoeing very shallow to avoid damaging the roots of roses and possibly causing suckers to grow from damaged parts.

Remove suckers now (see Chapter 6, Pruning), but don't confuse suckers with basal shoots, which often have a reddish tinge at this time of year.

If you plan to try some budding later on, be sure to obtain plants of the variety of understock used locally.

Late spring

Many roses will be at their best now, with masses of blooms and plenty of lush, healthy foliage to complement the flowers. Keep watching for basal shoots as they appear, gently encouraging them to grow in the desired direction by judicious staking and tying. Go over the bushes deadheading regularly; that is, removing spent flowers as they fade, always cutting above a five-leaflet leaf. Remove any twiggy growths throughout the season so the plant can concentrate its resources on flower-producing wood.

Now is the time to try some hybridising (see Chapter 7), and allow the heps to ripen if you want to collect the seed for next year.

Give the bushes a good feed after the first flowering, and this will enhance the next flush of flowers some 6-7 weeks later. Keep the soil moist by watering and applying a mulch if necessary.

Watch for signs of disease and remove all diseased leaves. Repeat the protective spraying, especially in humid areas. If a fungal disease gets away on you, it may be necessary to cut the plant back hard and remove all of the affected leaves to prevent the disease from spreading to other roses. If you do have to take this drastic action, no permanent harm will come to the plant as a result, so cut it back and decide whether you really want to retain that particular cultivar, or whether it might best be consigned to the incinerator and replaced with a more disease-resistant cultivar. If the latter is the case, remove the plant early in autumn or as soon as you are able.

Some keen gardeners will 'disbud' their Large-flowered roses. This means removing the side buds to allow the central flower to grow to its full potential.

Visit some spring rose shows if you can, and be sure to take a pen and paper to list the cultivars that you admire. Remember though that the roses exhibited may not necessarily be 'good doers' in the garden even though they look good on show benches. Make a few enquiries to see if the rose does well under ordinary garden conditions before you order. Another place to see roses en masse is in municipal gardens and in the display gardens of major rose nurseries, so see as many as possible to decide what you want to order for yourself for next season.

Keep an eye on cuttings and pot up any that have a good root system. Keep them moist and pot up to larger pots when the root mass nearly fills the pot. Small seedlings may also be in bud, and the excitement grows as they come into bloom.

Early summer

Keep the beds moist now, and top up the

Opposite: 'Pride of Hurst' (Polyantha)

'La Reine Victoria' (Bourbon)

mulch layer when necessary to keep the roots cool and to minimise evaporation of moisture from the soil. Water early in the day to allow the foliage to dry completely before nightfall. Rust may appear in humid areas, so check occasionally on the undersides of leaves for the tell-tale orange spots. Rust can completely defoliate a plant if it gets established, so when you're out picking blooms and zapping aphids, keep an eye out for diseases at the same time.

Hybridising can continue if you're keen to try your luck, and the heps will swell in a few weeks.

Blooms for decorative purposes should be cut early in the day if possible, or in the cool of the evening. Keep the petals from faded flowers, dry them and use for pot pourri and other delights (see Chapter 9).

Mid summer

Rose growers in warm and temperate districts now have an awful choice to make. Roses can be left to bloom as they choose until the end of the season, or they can be summer pruned, in which case you sacrifice some blooms now for the sake of a glorious autumn flush of blooms. If you decide to let them bloom at will, keep up the deadheading and watering and give the plants a good feed late in the month.

Keep up the protective spraying if necessary and watch for powdery mildew which occurs mainly where the air circulation is impeded.

If you decide to trim for a great autumn display, cut right back on watering from the end of the month and save the feeding for later. Cut blooms with only short stems from late in the month.

Roses in containers also need to be kept moist and this may mean daily watering depending on the weather and the position and size of the containers.

In hot, dry weather, you may see evidence of spider mites on the undersides of leaves, so remove the mites with a good, strong burst from the hose and discourage them by keeping the foliage well watered during the driest part of the year only. This is when the presence of the predator mite *Phytoseilus persimilis* will be appreciated.

Late summer

If you are letting the plants bloom at will, keep them well watered. If aiming for an autumn display, leave the plants unwatered unless conditions are excessively dry, in which case water as little as possible, as deep watering early this month will upset the timing of the autumn blooms. When removing faded blooms, only cut off the spent head at this time of year if you plan to summer trim, as this allows new growth to come high up on the stems. Then late in the month give the

A rose walk created with climbing roses.

plants the heaviest watering of the year, soaking them thoroughly. Follow with a light feeding, then another deep watering after that. A week or two later, go over all the canes on every plant and cut them just as though you were cutting long-stemmed blooms for the vase. It may be hard to bring yourself to do this, but if you have a special date in autumn in mind when you want the roses to be absolutely magnificent, then this is the way to do it, though it's not for the faint hearted!

Keep the soil moist to maintain rapid growth, and watch as usual for diseases. Your autumn blooms will appear around 7 weeks after this pruning, provided you do all the other things associated with the trim, like feeding and watering at the right times and provided, of course, that the season is reasonably 'normal' with regard to rain and temperature. Follow the trim with another generous feeding and watering, then apply a mulch to help provide the plants with everything they need for those autumn flowers. The warmth that the roses need to bloom will be there in the air and the soil, but you must supply the food and water.

Prune any roses flowering only in summer and give them some food to provide long canes for next year's blooms.

Early autumn

There will still be many blooms on bushes that have not been summer trimmed, and it's still worth deadheading and cutting blooms to allow for the appearance of more flowers in warm areas. Autumn blooms will come in greater abundance than the spring blooms as the bushes are much larger, and there may be autumn shows to visit in warm and temperate areas.

Keep watering bushes that have been sum-

Opposite: 'Cécile Brunner' (Polyantha)

mer trimmed and give them another feeding when flower buds emerge. It is well worth experimenting with the timing of the summer prune, as each district will be slightly different according to soil temperature and hours of sunlight. But after a year or two of practice, you should be able to time your autumn blooms to perfection for any date you select. New basal shoots should not be included in the trim as cutting into them in summer may kill them, but more mature basals can have their tips trimmed.

Watering will still be necessary in some parts as rain may not yet have been sufficient to keep the plants flowering well, but you will be able to judge this for yourself after a while and know when your plants need watering.

New basal shoots can appear at this time of year, and should always be staked and tied as they will harden and form the basis of the new season's growth.

Keep an eye out for powdery mildew as the nights are becoming cooler, and watch for caterpillars that may be feeding on the leaves. Aphids and katydids may also make an appearance, so be on the lookout and take appropriate action. Katydids will chew through new growth at a great rate and beetles can also do a lot of damage in autumn, but both can be hand-picked from the plants and destroyed.

At this time of year, decide on the bushes that you want to replace and dig them out well before winter if you can. Some that you personally don't like can be given away, but those being discarded because of disease problems should be burned. Dig out as much as possible of the root system and allow the space to remain empty until planting next season's choices.

Chapter 9

ROSES AS CUT FLOWERS

'Gold Bunny' (Cluster-flowered)

ROSES last well as cut flowers, provided that the right steps are taken when the blooms are cut, and that the blooms are conditioned well before being arranged in vases.

When you go into the garden to pick roses, take a good, sharp pair of secateurs and a bucket of tepid water. Try to pick flowers early in the morning while they are still fresh, or in the cool of the evening. As you pick each bloom, cut the stem to the length you want, always cutting to that critical five-leaflet leaf, with the bud eye in the leaf axil, to ensure that another bloom will follow. Don't cut the stems any longer than necessary, as this deprives the plant of part of its store of nutrients. Having cut the stem cleanly, hold each one under water while you recut a few millimetres from the base. This will ensure that no air lock remains in the stem to prevent water uptake. Then plunge each stem up to the calyx (that is the base of the flower) in water. Take the bucket inside and place it

somewhere cool and out of direct sunlight for a few hours to condition; overnight if that suits your purpose. Many people add a few drops of bleach to the water, while others add an aspirin, a teaspoon of sugar or glucose, or a commercial preparation to improve the keeping quality of the blooms. The aim is to prevent the entry of bacteria into the stems and to provide some nourishment for the blooms. Go over the stems at some stage and remove the thorns, which are a menace when you are putting the arrangement together!

Ensure that the vase you use for the arrangement is filled to the top with water to provide humidity, and that you top it up daily with fresh water. Keep the roses out of direct sun and try to keep them in a room that is reasonably cool. With such treatment, they will last very well. Large-flowered roses and those with many petals are likely to last longer than flowers with few petals, as the former retain their shape better, and so are more suited to floral arrangements which are required to last longer.

Floral art

If floral art appeals to you, then it is wise to have several plants of your favoured cultivars so that you will always have enough blooms for the type of arrangement you like. Some floral artists like to plunge the cut stems into water that has just boiled for about 9 seconds before putting them into tepid water to condition. For floral art that has to last, the Large-flowered roses provide depth in arrangements because of their high-pointed centres. However, some truly stunning arrangements can be made with the great trusses of Cluster-flowered roses.

A wide range of other flowers and foliage combine well with roses in floral arrangements. A good supply of that wonderful florists' standby, gypsophila, will never go amiss, and Queen Anne's lace is always a reliable contrast. Carnations, larkspurs, love-in-a-mist and snapdragons also go well. Consider, too, the trailing green or variegated foliage of ivy, long, fragrant trails of jasmine, and the lovely foliage of copper beech and some of the finer conifers. Try to match the size of the flowers you are blending with the type of arrangement you have in mind; use tiny flowers for posy bowls and bouquets, and for a more dramatic look in a larger arrangement, try tall spikes of gladioli and watsonia or the grandeur of large proteas. Remember to condition all flowers and foliage used before creating your arrangements.

Rose shows

When visiting rose shows, you may well consider that the roses in your garden are every bit as good as those being exhibited and you would be absolutely right. The cultivars on show are available from nurseries and yours will do just as well on the show bench as the prize winners. If you want to try exhibiting, obtain a schedule from the show secretary

Cutting blooms

three-leaflet leaf

always cut blooms above a five-leaflet leaf

five-leaflet leaf from which a new flower will come

and determine which classes you may enter as a novice; this will be clearly explained on the schedule, but if in doubt contact the secretary for more information.

At rose shows, there are classes for Decorative blooms, which are from one-quarter to half open; Exhibition blooms, from half to three-quarters open; and Fully open blooms, which must be past the three-quarters open stage. There are also classes for stems of Cluster-flowered roses, which may be divided into Small stems, which have no more than three flowers open; and Large stems, having four or more flowers open. However, individual classes will vary between rose societies, and rules are periodically updated. There will be classes for vases of roses and for old-fashioned roses in most shows, and there may be a class for locally-raised seedling roses.

Roses are given points for their shape, freshness, balance and foliage, so all of these

Opposite: 'Madame President' (Cluster-flowered)

features are important when exhibiting. Don't be afraid to enter some of your own roses in shows. Other exhibitors will help if they know you are a first-time exhibitor, and you will learn a great deal from watching experienced people prepare their exhibits.

Using the petals

When blooms have faded and are deadheaded, it seems a waste to throw out all those fragrant petals. Instead of consigning them to the compost heap, spread them out on newspaper in a sheltered place to dry. They can then be used to make potpourri and other fragrant articles to scent rooms, drawers and cupboards long after the rose season has ended.

Moist potpourri

For a long-lasting potpourri, layer rose petals and other fragrant flowers and foliage such as lavender, lemon verbena, carnations, heliotrope, rosemary and thyme, with layers of sea salt, common salt, citrus rind or powdered orris root as a fixative. Use a large container with a lid and keep adding layers until the container is filled. You could also add some essential oils of geranium or bergamot, and some ground cloves and spices like cinnamon and nutmeg. Leave the closed container in a cool place for a few weeks, then use the mix as you like. If, with time, it begins to lose its fragrance, add a few drops of brandy to revive it.

Rose petals can be used to scent notepaper and ink, to flavour jams, jellies and desserts, and you can make a very tolerable rose cologne with half a cup of petals in half a cup of vodka or isopropyl alcohol, leaving it for a week to brew.

Roses can be dried to use in winter arrangements too, simply by cutting them at the bud stage or when just beginning to open and hanging them upside down to dry in a well-ventilated place until they are thoroughly dried.

Chapter 10

SELECTION OF CULTIVARS

'Aotearoa' (Large-flowered)

ULTIMATELY, the selection of specific rose cultivars for any garden is best made by the gardener, as personal preference with regard to colour, shape, size and fragrance will differ from one person to another. However, the following lists of cultivars have been compiled from roses that are well known and grown worldwide, and have been chosen for their adaptability to a wide range of climates and growing conditions. Remember though that growing conditions can affect how a rose performs, and can also influence fragrance and flower colour, so find out which cultivars do well in your area, and regard the following list as a guide for those who want reliable cultivars to start their rose gardens.

Roses may be given different names in various countries. In these cases, the rose is known by an internationally known patent name, given here in brackets; the first three letters indicate the name of the breeder, for example MAC for McGredy, KOR for Kordes and MEI for Meilland.

The letters after the brief description of each rose denote the following: F, fragrant; D, significant disease resistance; S, M or L, plant size.

Large-flowered/Hybrid Teas

Alexander (HARlex) Bright vermilion double flowers on a tall, vigorous plant. FDL

Aotearoa (MACgenev) Palest pink, double flowers and semi-glossy foliage. FDL

April Hamer Large, shell-pink flowers, deeper at the edges, and fully double. FDL

Deep Secret/Mildred Scheel Large, deepest crimson, double flowers. FL

Diamond Jubilee Buff-yellow flowers, cupped and fully double. Leathery foliage. FM

Opposite: 'Gold Medal' (Large-flowered)

Double Delight (ANdeli) Pointed buds open to large, creamy-white blooms, deeply edged in carmine/cerise. FM/L

Fragrant Cloud/Duftwolke (TANellis) Large, coral/geranium-red blooms of good shape. FL

Gold Medal (AROyqueli) Pointed buds open to beautifully shaped flowers of deepest yellow, flushed with orange. FDL

Grandpa Dickson Large, deep yellow blooms with faintly pink edges. FDM/L

Ingrid Bergman (POULman) Dark red, double blooms on an upright plant. FDM

Just Joey Large, buff-orange/apricot flowers and glossy foliage. FDM/L

Loving Memory (KORgund) Huge, deep red flowers of good shape. FDL

Marijke Koopman Pointed buds in clusters open to medium pink blooms of classic shape. FDM

Mon Cheri (AROcher) Large, medium pink, double flowers suffused yellow at the base and deeper pink at petal edges. FDM

'Diamond Jubilee' (Large-flowered)

Opposite: 'Peace'/'Madame A. Meilland' (Large-flowered)

Pascali (LENip) Double, creamy-white flowers of classic shape. Dark green foliage. M

Peace/Mme. A. Meilland Huge, golden-yellow flowers edged rose-pink and fully double. FL

The Australian Bicentennial Medium to deep red blooms, borne singly. Glossy foliage. FDL

Touch of Class (KRIcarlo) Double, medium pink blooms, shaded creamy-coral. FL

Whisky Mac (TANky) Large, classically shaped, double flowers of bronze/yellow. Glossy foliage. FM

Cluster-flowered/Floribundas

Avalanche (JACav) Shapely, creamy-white blooms. Floriferous. FL

Above: 'Touch of Class' (Large-flowered)   *Below:* 'Iceberg' (Cluster-flowered)

Above: 'Playboy'/'Cheerio' (Cluster-flowered)

Right: 'Trumpeter' (Cluster-flowered)

French Lace (JAClace) Ivory blooms, faintly pinkish, with a classic shape. FDM

Friesia/Korresia Double blooms of clear yellow. Good as cut flowers. FDM

Iceberg (KORbin) Double, white blooms. Floriferous. Light green foliage. FL

Margaret Merril (HARkuly) High-centred, large, creamy-white blooms sometimes suffused blush. FDL

Playboy/Cheerio Clear orange, single blooms shaded bright red, gold reverse. FM

Priscilla Burton (MACrat) Carmine/pink/white splashes. Semi-double, large blooms in large trusses. DM

Rock 'n' Roll (MACfirwal) Orange-red blooms, edged yellow, in large clusters. DM/L

Sexy Rexy (MACrexy) Double blooms, medium/light pink, in large trusses. DM

Softly, Softly (HARkotur) Well-shaped double blooms, pale pink suffused peach. FDL

Strawberry Ice Double, creamy-white blooms edged pink. Good as a cut flower. DS/M

Trumpeter (MACtru) Orange-red, double blooms in profusion. DS

Modern Climbers

Bantry Bay Large flowers in clusters. Soft pink with bright pink reverse. FD

Compassion Large blooms of pinkish/apricot. Vigorous grower. FD

Dublin Bay (MACdub) Large, deep red blooms in abundance. FD

Golden Showers Daffodil-yellow, double blooms. Vigorous. F

Handel (MACha) Large, creamy blooms edged carmine. Floriferous. D

Below: 'Strawberry Ice' (Cluster-flowered)

Above: 'Sexy Rexy' (Cluster-flowered)

Schoolgirl Large, shapely, orange-apricot blooms. FD

Swan Lake Fully double, white blooms with centres tinged pink. F

Westerland (KORwest) Large grower with double, apricot-salmon blooms. FD

White Cockade Large, white, double blooms. Smaller grower. F

Zéphirine Drouhin Thornless, semi-double, rose-pink blooms in trusses. Vigorous. F

Miniatures/Patio roses

Beauty Secret Deep red with plentiful, well-shaped blooms. F

Jean Kenneally (TINeally) Well-shaped, apricot blooms. FD

Ko's Yellow (MACkosyel) Large, yellow blooms tinged pink. FD

Little Jackie (SAVor) Well-shaped flowers blended in almond/cream/orange. F

Below: 'Ko's Yellow' (Miniature) *Above:* 'Beauty Secret' (Miniature)

Little Scotch Straw-yellow/buff flowers in profusion. F

Magic Carrousel (MORrousel) White petals edged with red.

Mary Marshall Pointed buds, orange flowers with a yellow base. F

Minnie Pearl (SAVahowdy) Light pink flowers suffused creamy-yellow. FD

Pink Petticoat Larger grower with well-shaped coral-pink blooms. Vigorous.

Rainbow's End (SAValife) Deep yellow blooms edged red. D

Tracey Wickham Well-shaped, bright yellow blooms edged red. F

White Dream (LENblank) Well-shaped, double, white blooms. F

English Roses

Graham Thomas (AUSmas) Deepest yellow, double blooms with a cupped shape. F

Mary Rose (AUSmary) Double blooms, medium pink and cupped. F

'Golden Wings' (Shrub)

Opposite: 'Mary Rose' (English)

Wenlock (AUSwen) Deep crimson, cupped blooms. FD

Shrub roses

Many other roses, some of them old-fashioned types, are suited to growing in the same way as the English Roses, that is, as shrubs, and will attain their own informal shape. Prune them lightly if you want to retain this shape, and use them mixed with other garden plants, or as hedges and for background plantings.

Eyeopener (INTerop) Small, semi-double flowers of medium red, with prominent yellow stamens. Dense, spreading growth. D

Golden Wings Large, single, gold blooms with prominent stamens. Hardy. F

Lavender Dream (INTerlav) Semi-double blooms of deep lilac in clusters. Floriferous.

Above: 'Blanc Double de Coubert' (Rugosa)   *Below:* 'Buff Beauty' (Hybrid Musk)

Sparrieshoop Pointed buds and single flowers of pale pink with wavy edges. Large. F

Old-fashioned roses

All of those listed here are fragrant to a degree. Sizes are not given as pruning methods and growing conditions can determine the size and shape of most old-fashioned roses.

Albertine [Rambler] Light-pink blooms suffused gold.

Ballerina [Hybrid Musk] Large trusses of single pink flowers.

Blanc Double de Coubert [Rugosa] Purest white, semi-double blooms.

Buff Beauty [Hybrid Musk] Rich, apricot-yellow blooms in clusters.

Cécile Brunner [Polyantha Hybrid] Beautifully shaped, tiny flowers of palest silvery-pink.

Duchesse de Brabant [Tea] Cupped, double blooms of clear pink. Blooms very early.

Frau Dagmar Haastrup [Rugosa] Large, single, light-pink blooms.

'Swany' (Ground cover)

Jean Ducher [Tea] Cupped, salmon-pink flowers, suffused yellow.

Madame Alfred Carrière [Noisette Climber] Clusters of globular, pinkish-white blooms.

Madame Isaac Periere [Bourbon] Huge, cupped blooms of crimson/purple.

Madame Legras de Saint Germaine [Alba] Snowy-white blooms flushed yellow in the centre.

Madame Pierre Oger [Bourbon] Cupped blooms of palest pink.

***Rosa rugosa* 'Alba'** [Rugosa] Large, white, single blooms with prominent stamens and heps.

Roseraie de l'Häy [Rugosa hybrid] Large, semi-double, crimson purple flowers.

Souvenir de la Malmaison [Bourbon (Climber or Bush)] Quartered, blush-pink blooms. Vigorous.

Wedding Day [Rambler] Profuse clusters of single, white flowers.

Ground-cover roses

Many Ramblers can be used to cover banks and large areas of ground in mild climates,

however, there are newer roses being bred with the ground-cover purpose in mind, intended for covering smaller areas.

Angelita (MACangeli) Compact plant with creamy-white flowers tinged pink. Good in pots.

Flower Carpet Pink (NOAtraum) and **Flower Carpet White** (NOAschnee) Both are vigorous growers that repeat flower all season. Suitable for containers. D (F white only)

Grouse (KORimro) Single blooms of light pink on a spreading, vigorous plant. F

Nozomi Single, pearl-pink, small flowers in trusses. Spreads freely.

Swany (MEIburenac) Very double flowers of purest white. Vigorous.

Rose trial grounds exist worldwide, in order to assess how new cultivars perform under local conditions. The roses' performances are judged according to strict guidelines. If you are able to visit local trial grounds, you will be able to see for yourself the newer roses, and find out which ones have gained awards. Trial ground awards will often ensure commercial viability for individual roses, and are highly prized by commercial hybridisers.

Rose societies also review new cultivars, and will often publish lists of the most popular roses as judged by their members, the majority of whom grow roses for garden display and picking, as well as for exhibiting. If you see a new rose doing well in local reviews, it is certainly worth a try in your garden, especially if it is proving disease resistant, a significant characteristic, and one to be sought by all rose growers. Try some newer cultivars from time to time and, in general, give a new rose three full years to mature before you make up your mind one way or the other about it. It is from these new cultivars that tomorrow's classics and most popular roses will come, and there's nothing like a new rose or two each year to keep your addiction alive and well!

Approximate metric conversions

To Convert	to	Multiply by
metres (m)	feet	3.28
centimetres (cm)	inches	0.40
millimetres (mm)	inches	0.04
cubic metres (m³)	cubic yards	1.31
litres (l)	gallons (US)	0.26
litres (l)	gallons (Imp)	0.22
grams (g)	ounces	0.24
kilograms (kg)	pounds	2.20

GLOSSARY

Bare root roses. Roses bought without any soil around their roots; usually in plastic bags and usually available only in winter.

Basal shoot/water shoot. A shoot growing from above the bud union, forming the framework for subsequent years' growth.

Bud union/bud head. The place at which the scion is budded onto the rootstock.

Budding/budding on. The method of inserting growth buds from a wanted cultivar into the bark of a rootstock.

Clone. A plant propagated from the tissue of the parent, i.e., through tissue culture, layering or by cutting.

Cultivar. Short for 'cultivated variety.' A variety of rose raised in cultivation. Not a species rose.

Damping off. A fungus disease that causes seedlings to wither and die. Spray to prevent with a very weak solution of cupric hydroxide.

Dead-heading. Removing spent flower heads to encourage new flowers.

Die back. The slow dying back of a cane, usually from a pruning cut.

Eye/bud eye/growth eye. Small amount of tissue growing between the stem and a leaf. The part used to bud onto rootstock.

Friable (of soil). Able to be worked. The rule of thumb is that if some soil is squeezed in the hand it will retain its shape when released but still crumble when touched.

Hep/hip. Rose seed pods, usually yellow, orange or red when ripened.

Heeling in. Temporary planting of roses.

Humus. Decomposed organic matter essential to the life of the soil.

Mulch. A layer of material laid over beds to conserve moisture, reduce summer temperatures and suppress weed growth. Can be inorganic, e.g., polythene, but more often organic, e.g., bark, compost, sawdust, seaweed, grass clippings, etc.

Repeat flowering/recurrent/remontant. The ability of a cultivar to flower again in the same season after the first flush of bloom.

Rootstock. The plant onto which the wanted cultivar is budded. Rootstocks are selected for their vigour and disease resistance.

Scion. The cultivar which is budded onto the rootstock.

Soil biota. All soil dwelling organisms, including earthworms, fungi and bacteria.

Species. A wild rose; one not raised through cultivation; not a hybrid.

Sport. A mutation; a shoot that is different in some way from the parent plant. Growth eyes or cuttings from the mutant shoot may be used to propagate the sport.

Sucker. Growth arising from below the bud union. In budded plants, the sucker will be from the rootstock and should be removed; in cloned plants, the sucker can be used for propagation or allowed to grow, making a bushier plant.

Understock. See rootstock.

Variety. See cultivar.

'April Hamer' (Large-flowered)

Acknowledgements

My grandparents, Lizzie Edith Curthoys and John William Tobias grew the first roses I knew, and the spell of those roses is with me still.

My family has always indulged my love affair with roses, and I thank them for that.

Travis Flint, who first insisted that I write about roses, is a constant source of wisdom, delight and enthusiastic argument on the many aspects of rose growing, and I admire his strength and tenacity.

Allan Munro, Managing Editor of *New Zealand Growing Today* gave permission to adapt articles that first appeared in that publication.

The staff of Egmont Roses (New Zealand) and Malanseuns (South Africa) assisted in the selection of cultivars to include.

Ron Bell loaned his photographs of 'April Hamer'.

Emma Harding told me what beginners need to know about roses, and helped greatly with photography.

Many people allowed me to take photographs in their gardens. Among these were Judy and David Haigh, June and Laurie Bell, Alan Sinclair and Theo Verryt of 'Roseneath', and Frank Schuurman. Other photographs were taken at the Parnell Rose Gardens and at the Manurewa Rose Trial Grounds, in Auckland, and at Brundretts nursery in Melbourne.

Lastly, my husband John gave the endless help and support that made this book possible.

Janet Cheriton

INDEX